FROM STAR
TO SUPERSTAR

From Star *to* Superstar

the

ASIAN AMERICAN GUIDE TO ELITE COLLEGES

Barbara Austin, PhD

COLLEGE QUEST PRESS

This book is intended for informational purposes only and does not guarantee admission or scholarship outcomes. Every student's journey is different. The views expressed are those of the author based on over 30 years of college admissions experience. Always consult directly with colleges or professionals when making high-stakes decisions.

The students featured in this book have generously allowed me to share their essays so that you can study them, extract the elements that resonate with you, and craft something uniquely your own.

FROM STAR TO SUPERSTAR
The Asian American Guide to Elite Colleges
Copyright © 2026 by Barbara Austin

Printed in the United States of America

College Quest Press
693 Jean Street
Oakland, California 94610
college-quest.com

LCCN: 2025919016
ISBN: 979-8-9998784-2-7

*This book took me 20 years to write and
I dedicate it to all my students and their parents.
Thank you for teaching me so much so thoroughly.*

Table of Contents

PART II
Rising to Superstar

PART III
Proving Your Superstar Status

Introduction

The phone call came in May, just three weeks before the end of the student's junior year. A Chinese mother was asking for help. Her daughter had a 4.0 GPA and a 1520 SAT score. She played piano beautifully, sang in competitions, and was trying to start a food-service fundraiser. She'd been rejected from three summer programs but had gotten into Boston University's three-week STEM course. Would singing at senior centers help her chances for Early Decision at Pomona?

My heart sank. I could picture this girl studying relentlessly for those perfect grades—the countless hours of SAT prep, the amazing focus, the discipline and motivation. I guessed that she didn't date, that she led a quiet, disciplined life focused entirely on excellence.

And I hated being the one to tell her—that's not enough.

Because here's the truth: You can't decide to focus only on grades and tests for three years, then miraculously become interesting in your last few months of high school. The path to standing out starts much earlier.

Numbers, data, test scores—these make you eligible. But to get into elite colleges today, you need something more than being a star. You need a story that makes you a superstar. And for Asian American students facing unofficial quotas and unconscious bias, that story needs to be unforgettable.

I've spent thirty years helping Asian American students get into America's most selective colleges—not by teaching them to hide their identity or become someone else, but by helping them discover and develop what makes them genuinely remarkable.

In the following pages, I'll show you

+ why perfect numbers aren't enough anymore;

+ how to create something truly remarkable;

+ how to make your story unforgettable; and

+ which elite colleges will value your unique excellence and accept you.

And I'll use examples of real students to show you exactly how *they* did it.

The path to being a superstar does exist, and my students will show you how to follow that path. But you need to start now!

Learning to See

When I first began working with Asian American students, I was amazed. Their focus, discipline, and raw capability exceeded anything I'd seen in my years of teaching at community and four-year colleges or volunteering at multiple high schools in the San Francisco Bay Area. But something was missing.

These brilliant students knew parts of the college admissions game, but not all of it. They could solve complex math problems but struggled to tell their own stories. They pursued academic excellence relentlessly, but they often left their hearts behind.

And their parents? They watched me carefully, as they should. I remember Peter's mother insisting that we meet at her local library, which was an hour away. Then, for two hours, she had me explain every point of the "star framework," probing for weaknesses, making sure that I wasn't just another consultant with empty promises. She needed to know that her son would be in good hands.

Then there was the father who kept interrupting his daughter during our story development session. Finally the truth emerged—he had suffered greatly in China before immigrating to the US. The idea of his daughter mining that pain for an essay was unthinkable to him. Some stories, I learned, are too precious to share.

Trust in my guidance developed slowly, earned through hard work (no shortcuts, no gimmicks), research (knowing that every detail matters), insight (understanding what *wasn't* said), and consistency (being there for every step). And finally there were the results—one success leading to another!

When my students began getting into top schools in competitive majors, parents told their friends. Their friends told neighbors. Soon I couldn't help everyone who asked. But as I worked with more Asian American families, I began to recognize patterns that weren't apparent at first, either to me or to most parents and students. Four key concepts emerged that explained why even exceptional Asian American students often face unexpected challenges.

THE ASIAN TAX. Research from Princeton University revealed a disturbing reality: Asian American students need SAT scores approximately 100 points higher than their peers from other backgrounds to have equal chances of admission.[1] Like a tax levied simply for being Asian, this higher standard creates an unspoken barrier that raw numbers alone cannot overcome.

THE VILLAIN OF KNOWLEDGE. Admissions officers, overwhelmed by thousands of applications, unconsciously stereotype applicants—"another piano prodigy with perfect

---

1. Espenshade, Thomas J., and Alexandria Walton Radford, *No Longer Separate, Not Yet Equal: Race and Class in Elite College Admission and Campus Life* (Princeton University Press, 2009), 92–93.

scores" or "another STEM student with robotics competitions." This presumption of knowing an applicant's story before actually reading it particularly affects Asian American students.

THE FIFTEEN MINUTES OF FAME. Each college application receives approximately fifteen minutes of review time. In that brief window, students must not only present their accomplishments but also overcome stereotypes and truly connect with the readers.

LIKE CANCELS LIKE. When thousands of Asian applicants present similar profiles—excellent grades, high test scores, similar extracurriculars—they effectively cancel each other out. Even extraordinary achievements can seem ordinary when numerous applicants share similar backgrounds.

Understanding these hidden rules (see Appendix 1, page 283) changed everything about how I approached college admissions coaching. It wasn't enough to help students achieve excellence; they needed to achieve *distinctive* excellence in ways that overcame the systemic challenges.

These students didn't need to be fixed or changed. They needed to be *seen*—really seen. They needed help uncovering the stories they already had, developing the talents they kept private, and finding the best colleges to value their unique voice. And that is why I wrote this book.

Every immigrant family that walks through my door carries generations of dreams. Getting into an elite college is, above all, aspirational—to change the course of history and opportunity for their families. My job isn't to remake those dreams; it's to help make them possible.

CHAPTER 2

Be the Red—
Standing Out Authentically

In ancient Rome, a philosopher named Agrippinus was invited to one of Nero's grand banquets. When he declined—not just declined, but said he hadn't even considered attending—another philosopher asked him why. Most people, Agrippinus explained, see themselves like threads in a garment. They try to match the other threads in color and style, believing their job is to blend in perfectly with the whole. But Agrippinus saw things differently. "I want to be the red," he said, "that small and brilliant portion which causes the rest to appear comely and beautiful. 'Be like the majority of people?' And if I do that, how shall I any longer be the red?"

The Agrippinus story captures perfectly the challenge facing Asian American students today. Let me explain why.

The Blending Trap

Every week I meet brilliant students who have done everything "right." They've earned perfect GPAs in the most rigorous courses, received President's Volunteer Service Awards (gold level, of course), and music certificates through Level 10. They've held positions as club treasurer or secretary, founded anime or baobab fundraising clubs, and contributed extensive volunteer hours at food banks and libraries, along with earning Eagle Scout achievements or Girl Scout Gold Awards.

These are impressive accomplishments. They represent years of hard work, discipline, and dedication. But here's the painful truth: When every thread matches perfectly, none of them stand out. When everyone has the same gold medals, they cease to shine.

Let me show you what I mean. A few years ago, I worked with three students **from different high schools** who were applying to the University of California, Berkeley.

— All had 4.0+ GPAs.

— All had 1500+ SAT scores.

— All were officers in their school Red Cross Club or math or computer science club.

— All had Gold President's Volunteer Service Awards.

— All wanted to major in STEM subjects—premed, business, computer science, or engineering.

Like threads in the same garment, they canceled each other out. "Like cancels like" is one of the most painful realities of college admissions, especially for Asian American students competing against each other.

The Authenticity Solution

But there's another way. As brilliant entrepreneur Naval Ravikant says, "Escape competition through authenticity." This is what Cathy understood. Yes, she played the piano, but instead of just earning more certificates, she created "Little Chopins" and taught music to underserved elementary students. Her love of music became a bridge to service and leadership.

This is what Peter grasped too. Rather than just excel in band, he developed an iOS app that transformed how his orchestra practiced. His passion for music merged with his interest in technology to create something genuinely new.

And this is what Angela discovered. Instead of forcing herself to excel in subjects that drained her, she built her path around what energized her: writing and literature. She became editor in chief of both her school's newspaper and its literary magazine, won scholastic writing awards, and got into competitive summer creative writing programs. Even more importantly, when her city sought a high school poet laureate, they found her with poems in hand. When Barnard College accepted her Early Decision application, they weren't getting another "perfect" Asian American student—they were getting a genuine literary voice.

Finding Your Red

"Being the red" doesn't mean being loud or flashy. It means

— having the courage to be authentically yourself;

— *creating* rather than just achieving;

— making contributions that only you can make; and

— standing out through genuine excellence.

One of my favorite students was Michelle, who loved to crochet. When she started working with me, she had a 4.5 average GPA and a 1560 SAT score, and she loved to crochet gifts for her family and friends. By the time she left for the University of Chicago, she had started a project at Stanford University where she taught mothers-to-be how to crochet baby blankets. In addition, together with twenty other members in her crocheting club, she started making hundreds of crocheted blankets to raise thousands of dollars for unwed mothers.

The secret isn't trying to become someone else—it's becoming more fully *yourself*. Throughout my thirty years helping Asian American students get into elite colleges, I've discovered that the path to standing out isn't through competition but through authenticity.

This book will show you how to

— move beyond trying to match others' expectations;

— transform private excellence into public impact;

— create something genuinely remarkable;

— tell your unique story in a compelling way; and

— find colleges that value your authentic self and story.

The Path Forward

In the chapters ahead, I'll share the process I've developed over three decades, helping students move from being stars (impressive but potentially invisible) to being superstars—authentically unforgettable.

Here's what's key: You don't get yourself into college—it's your *story* that gets you in. Colleges don't have the time or personnel to interview each student. For example, University of California schools accept no recommendations or interviews; instead, everything is focused on the story your application tells.

The most compelling stories don't come from trying to match everyone else. They come from having the courage to "be the red"—that small but brilliant portion that stands out not through competition but through authentic excellence.

Let's get started.

CHAPTER 3

Building Your Dream College— Blueprint for Success

*"Put the center in the right place,
and the circle draws itself perfectly."*
—MEISTER ECKHART

Let me show you how to build your dream college—not by following everyone else's blueprint but by creating one that showcases your unique story.

Your Dream College

The Foundation

Getting into your dream college starts with…

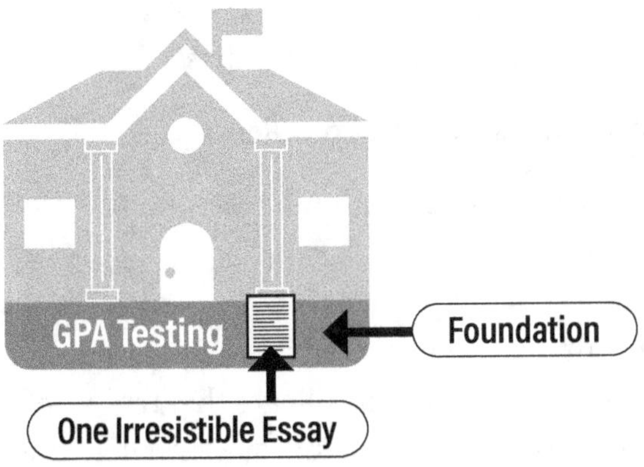

— A strategic GPA—not just high grades,
   but the right courses

— Test scores (if they are required)

— One irresistible essay that makes colleges care

The Windows

In each window sits a star. These stars represent what colleges truly seek: students who will light up the campus. But being a star isn't about perfection. It's about all these things:

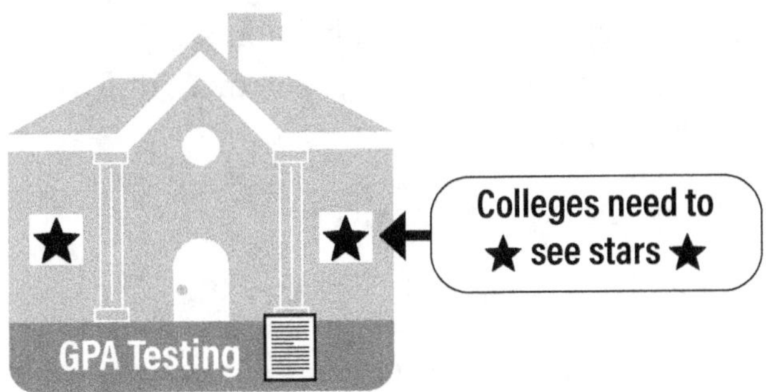

— Leadership that makes a difference

— Talent developed into contribution

— Service that shows genuine compassion

— Initiative that solves real problems

— Academic excellence with purpose

The Door

Entrance to your dream college isn't through numbers alone. The door opens when you find colleges that truly "get" your story—institutions where your unique excellence will be recognized and valued.

The Wheel of Success

At the center of every successful application sits your own irresistible story. Like spokes on a wheel, everything connects back to this core:

— Service that shows your impact

— Recommendations that validate your story

— Interviews that make your journey come alive

— Essays that make admissions officers emotionally care

— Leadership that demonstrates your value

When your story sits at the center, everything else aligns naturally. Each element of your application doesn't just show what you've done; it reveals who you are and what you'll bring to the campus.

Where Are You Now?

Before you start the journey to becoming unforgettable to colleges, it's important to know where you stand. That's why we begin with the "star" inventory—a clear-eyed look at your current strengths and opportunities.

In the chapters ahead, you'll learn how to do all these things:

— Assess your current star status

— Strengthen each point of your star

— Move from star to superstar by doing the following:

+ Create something remarkable

+ Craft "sticky" essays

+ Build powerful recommendations

+ Find your perfect college matches

Remember: Every superstar starts as a "regular" star. Let's begin by seeing exactly where you are and how far you can go.

KEY INSIGHTS:

+ Put your irresistible story at the center, and everything else will align naturally.

+ Every element of your application should reveal not just what you've done, but who you are.

+ You're building your dream college with every choice you make, so be sure you're building one that you'll want to live in.

PART I

The Star Foundation

CHAPTER 4

Taking Your Star Inventory

Before you can become a superstar, you need to know where you stand as a star. Think of this chapter as your personal GPS, showing you exactly where you are on your college journey.

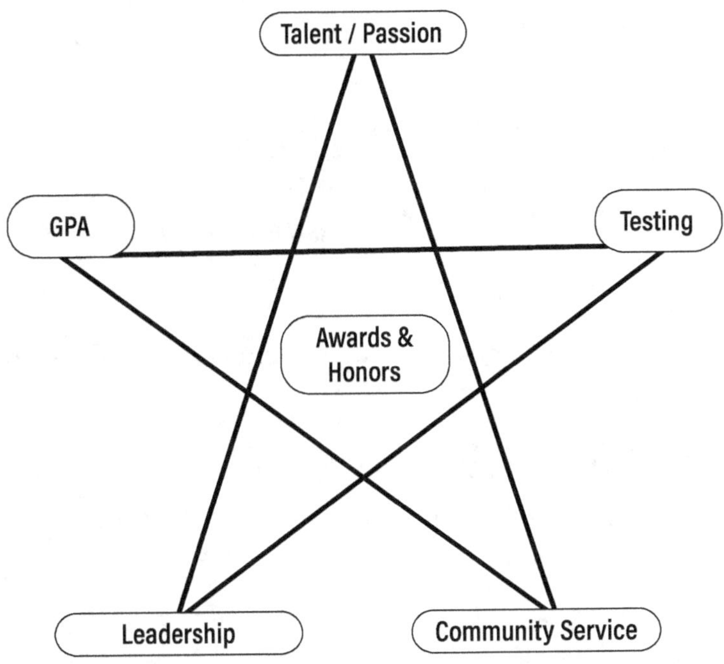

Let's take a close look at each point of your own star. To begin, get out a piece of paper and draw a large five-pointed star on it. This star represents you—two arms, two legs, and your head at the top. Now let's fill it in together.

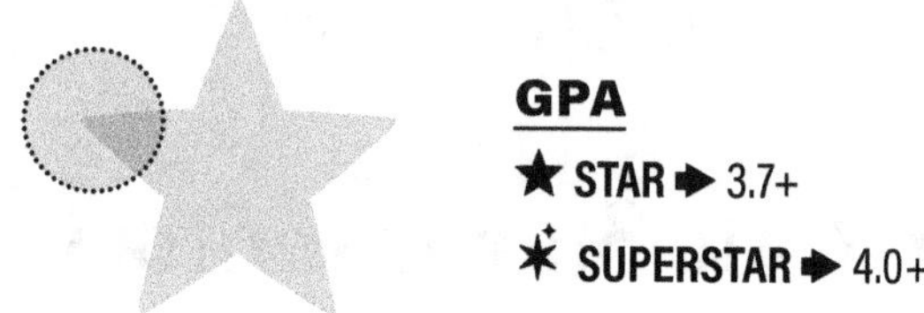

Left arm: your GPA. This is your foundation. Write your current unweighted GPA here.

— Star level: 3.7+ unweighted

— Superstar level: 4.0 unweighted, with **Golden 20 curriculum** (see Kabir's story in Chapter 5, p. 31)

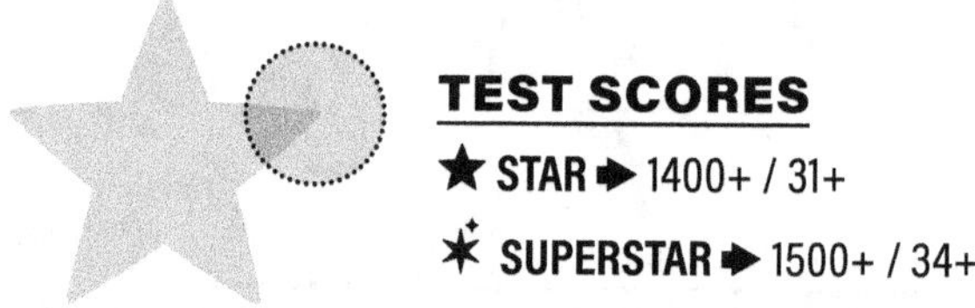

Right arm: test scores. Write down your current SAT/ACT/PSAT scores.

— Star level: 1400+ SAT / 31+ ACT

— Superstar level: 1500+ SAT / 34+ ACT / National Merit Finalist

TALENT / PASSION

★ **STAR** ➡ Excellence in one area

✳ **SUPERSTAR** ➡ Excellence with significant contribution/awards

Top point: talent/passion. List your main talents and genuine interests.

— Star level: demonstrated excellence in one area

— Superstar level: excellence with significant contribution/awards

LEADERSHIP

★ **STAR** ➡ Active leadership in one or two clubs

✳ **SUPERSTAR** ➡ Leadership and initiative that creates lasting difference

Left leg: leadership. List your leadership roles and initiatives.

— Star level: active leadership in one or two organizations

— Superstar level: creating lasting difference through your leadership

SERVICE

★ **STAR** ➡ Consistent involvement
in one or two causes

✳ **SUPERSTAR** ➡ Created or transformed
service that contributed to school
or community

Right leg: service. List your volunteer work and community involvement.

— Star level: consistent involvement in one or
two causes

— Superstar level: created or transformed service
opportunities that contributed to school or
community

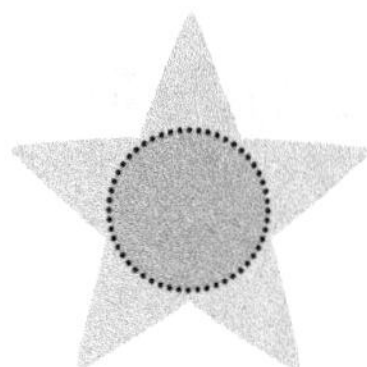

AWARDS / HONORS

★ **STAR** ➡ School or local recognition

✳ **SUPERSTAR** ➡ Regional, state,
or national recognition

Center: awards and honors. List any recognition you've received.

— Star level: school or local recognition

— Superstar level: regional, state, or national
recognition

Meet Emily, a Star in Progress

Here's how this process worked with a real student. When Emily first came to me, her star looked like this:

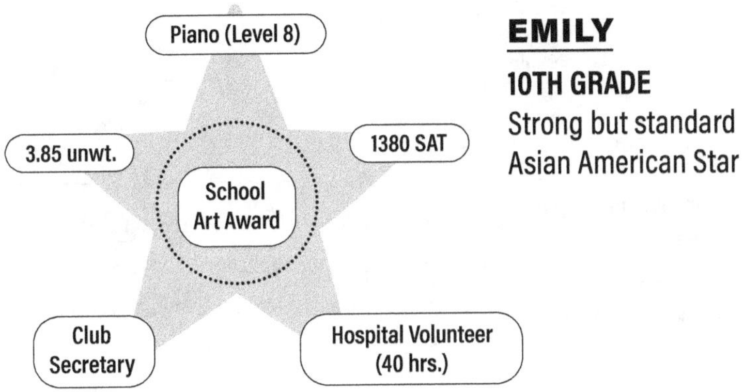

— Left arm: 3.85 unweighted

— Right arm: 1380 SAT

— Top point: piano (Level 8)

— Left leg: club secretary

— Right leg: hospital volunteer (40 hours)

— Center: school art award

Emily was a classic "strong but standard" Asian American applicant—good, but not yet distinctive enough for elite colleges. Like many students I meet, she had the foundation for excellence but hadn't yet found her unique way to shine.

Now take a look at where Emily ended up after following the strategies you'll learn in this book:

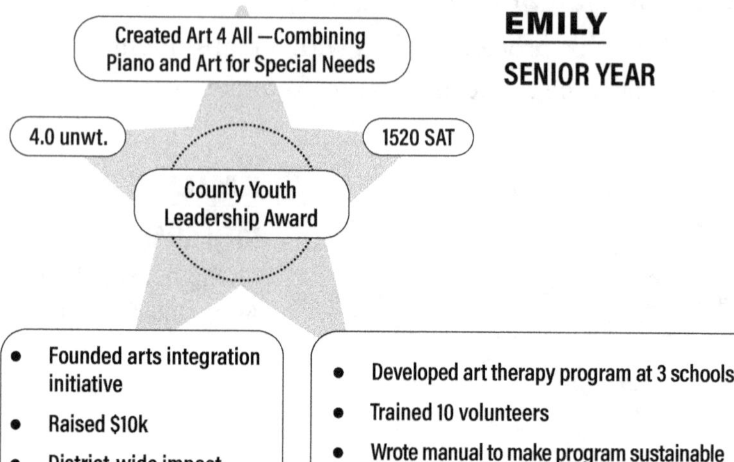

— Left arm: 4.0 unweighted. She found her rhythm in AP classes by choosing subjects that energized her and by getting help early when needed.

— Right arm: 1520 SAT. She approached test prep strategically, focusing on her strengths and treating it like a game she could master.

— Top point: created "Art 4 All." She transformed her private artistic excellence into public impact by teaching special needs students and combining piano and art in therapy programs at three elementary schools.

— Left leg: founded an arts integration initiative. Leading a team of fifteen students, she raised $10,000 for arts education and made a district-wide impact.

— Right leg: developed an art therapy program. She created and launched a program at three schools, trained ten other student volunteers, and wrote a manual for them to make the program sustainable.

— Center: earned a County Youth Leadership Award. She received recognition for her arts integration initiative, was featured in local media, and saw her program become a model for other schools.

The result? Early Decision acceptance to Brown University to study education and public policy, while also running the school's "Arts in Action" program.

Mapping Your Own Star

Take fifteen minutes right now to do the following:

1. Complete your own star diagram.

2. Circle your strong points in green.

3. Circle any areas needing development in red.

4. Write down an initial action plan to improve what's missing.

Now make a quick check for each point on your star:

— Are you at star level yet?

— What's the next step toward superstar level?

— What resources do you need to make that happen?

Why This Matters

Emily's transformation wasn't magic. By following the same steps you'll learn in these pages, she was able to

— build on her own genuine interests;

— make strategic choices;

— create a team to help her;

— find ways to contribute; and

— create lasting change.

By creating the art therapy program and writing the corresponding manual, Emily's work is still humming along years after she graduated!

As author Tim Ferriss notes in his popular podcast, success leaves clues. Whenever he needs to do something difficult, he looks up how someone else did it successfully before him, and then he follows in that path.

Success leaves clues—that's what this book is about. And my students have left clues for you to follow. Emily left clues for you, just as all the other students in this book have done. I'm simply revealing what has succeeded, and why.

In the following pages, we'll take each point of the star and show how to develop it, just as Emily did. First we'll help you *become* a star. Then we'll show you how to transform yourself into a superstar. Ready to begin your transformation? Turn the page!

KEY INSIGHTS:

✦ Success leaves clues. The students in this book have left clues for you to follow.

✦ The star is your personal college GPS—it will show you exactly where you are on your college journey.

Star Assessment Worksheet

Name:

Grade:

Date:

GPA Assessment

Current unweighted GPA: _______

Star level (3.7+)? _______   Superstar level (4.0+)? _______

Test Scores

SAT: _______   ACT: _______   PSAT: _______

Star level (1400+ / 31+)? _______

Superstar level (1500+ / 34+)? _______

Talent/Passion

Main talents/interests: _______

How are you using them to contribute? _______

____

Star level? _______   Superstar level? _______

Leadership

Current roles: _______

Star level? _______   Superstar level? _______

Your Dream College— The GPA Foundation

There's a story about an architect who spent his entire life building magnificent homes for others. When he was ready to retire, the king begged him to build one final house. Tired and ready to be finished, the architect cut corners, used cheaper materials, and rushed the job. When he finished, the king smiled and handed him the keys. "This is your house," the king said. "Your retirement gift."

The architect stood there heartbroken. If only he had known that he was building his own house.

Here's the truth: You're building your dream college while you're in high school. Every class choice, every hour of study, every decision is either building toward that dream or moving away from it. But remember, there's more than one way to build excellence.

Two Paths to Excellence

Meet Olivia and Kabir. They are students who built two very different houses, but they both found their perfect homes.

OLIVIA: BUILDING WITH FOCUS. While other students wear themselves down trying to excel at everything, Olivia found her own path to rigor—one that energized rather than drained her. Rather than forcing herself through Calculus BC or obsessing over SAT math, she instead

— became editor in chief of her school's literary magazine;

— won scholastic writing awards;

— took AP Spanish (along with Mandarin);

— led the school newspaper as managing editor; and

— got into competitive writing programs.

Her SAT score wasn't perfect (780 reading, 675 math), but it was strategic. Her GPA didn't include all A's in the most advanced classes, but she excelled where it mattered for achieving her own goals. The result? Early Decision acceptance to Wesleyan as an English major with a creative writing minor—a perfect match to amplify her kind of excellence.

KABIR: BUILDING FOR THE STARS. Kabir understood something different: To get into Stanford, he needed the strongest possible foundation. He built his dream with the "Golden 20"—the most rigorous possible course load— which meant taking

— four years of English (ending in AP);

— four years of history/social science (ending in AP History, AP Economics);

— four years of language (strategically choosing Spanish over Mandarin);

— four years of science (full sequence of AP Biology, AP Chemistry, AP Physics A and C); and

— four years of math (through Calculus BC).

But here's what made Kabir truly smart: He found his own path to academic rigor. When his school couldn't provide what he needed, he instead

— studied Spanish through an outside program;

— added political science at a community college because his high school wasn't strong in AP social sciences;

— pursued multivariable calculus beyond BC; and

— never blinked at taking hard classes, such as AP US History and AP Physics, creating study groups to tackle the toughest courses.

Kabir knew that getting A's in the Golden 20 made him eligible for Stanford. But getting *into* Stanford was a whole different ball game. Here's what both Olivia and Kabir understood: It's not about becoming an "AP machine." Some Asian American students pile up APs until their weighted GPA hits 4.9, or they self-study just to take AP tests. This can be a trap. Why? Because of the following:

— Elite colleges value genuine engagement over raw numbers.

— The University of California system currently only counts four full-year AP classes in a student's GPA. Only AP courses taken the summer after ninth grade through the summer after eleventh grade are considered for the GPA calculation (this includes honors and IB courses).

— Self-studied APs without labs or real classroom experience don't impress.

— Time spent chasing more APs could be better used developing leadership and contributions.

Your Blueprint for Success

★ STAR PATH (like Olivia):

— A strong foundation (4.0 GPA in key areas)

— Strategic excellence in your particular strengths

— Focused rigor where it matters most

✦ SUPERSTAR PATH (like Kabir):

— Golden 20 foundation

— Strategic additions beyond the school's courses

— Balance between rigor and real engagement

Now take a look at your current high school classes and activities. Mark each as being one of these:

E = Energizing

D = Draining

B = Blinking (avoiding hard classes)

The E's are showing you your path. The D's show where you might be building someone else's dream college instead of your own. The B's show where you've decided *not* to go to the next level.

Final Truths

1. Always go to the next level—but do so strategically.

2. Don't become an AP machine just to boost your numbers.

3. Remember: You become eligible with grades, but you get in with heart.

4. Build where your energy is greatest.

5. Match with colleges that value your kind of excellence.

Most importantly, don't be like that architect mentioned at the start of this chapter, building without purpose. Whether you're following the path of Olivia's focused excellence or Kabir's comprehensive rigor, build *intentionally*. Each academic decision you make in high school adds another brick to your dream college. Make sure you're building one you'll want to live in.

KEY INSIGHTS:

+ There's more than one path to academic excellence. Find the one that energizes rather than drains you.

+ Strategic rigor matters more than collecting AP classes. Choose depth over breadth.

+ Build your foundation intentionally. Every class choice adds another brick to your dream college.

CHAPTER 6

Understanding the Testing Game

Jeffrey, one of my students, learned a crucial lesson about standardized testing in a most unexpected way. He and his teammates were competing at a DECA international competition in a hotel simulation event. Despite months of preparation and running what they thought was a nearly perfect hotel, they found themselves stuck in seventh place after the first round.

That night, frustrated but determined, Jeffrey had a revelation: They weren't supposed to run an actual hotel, they were supposed to win a simulation. There's a crucial difference. For the second round, they completely changed their approach. Instead of trying to run the most realistic hotel, they focused solely on what the simulation valued—overall sales over profit. They stripped away all creative thinking and human judgment, treating it purely as a system of coding that every customer, employee, and manager followed. The result? They won first place!

What the SAT Really Values

Let me explain something crucial about standardized testing that most students (and many prep programs) don't understand. In many Asian countries, particularly China, everything rides on a single test: the Gaokao. This test can make or break a student's future. Millions of students compete for very limited spots at elite universities based purely on this one exam, which helps explain why many immigrant families focus so intensely on test scores.

But the SAT is a different kind of game entirely. Like Jeffrey's hotel simulation, it values some very specific things:

1. Economical use of one's time

    Smart time management is of paramount importance—the test is designed to punish perfectionism. You get the same points for easy questions as for hard ones, so five minutes spent struggling with one difficult problem could cost you three easy questions.

2. Strategic guessing over accuracy

    The Princeton Review, the excellent SAT prep service, uses an insightful image to illustrate the power of strategic guessing on the SAT: Imagine that every right answer on the SAT gets you a dollar and every wrong answer only costs you twenty-five cents. This means you can safely guess, because you're only penalized twenty-five cents if you get it wrong, but you get a full dollar if you get it right. Studies show that young men often score higher on the SAT than young women— not because they know more, but because they're more willing to do strategic guessing.

3. Pattern recognition over deep knowledge

   The SAT is deliberately designed with traps and sinkholes. Some questions are nearly impossible to answer correctly—the test makers do this on purpose! Success comes from recognizing patterns and question types. It's about playing the game, not showcasing your intelligence.

The Digital SAT: A New Game with New Rules

Since 2023, the SAT has gone digital and adaptive, changing the game in important ways. Like Jeffrey had to adjust his strategy for the DECA competition, you'll need to adjust your approach for this new format.

The Adaptive Structure

The digital SAT is now adaptive. Each subject (Reading & Writing, Math) is split into two modules. Your performance in the first module determines the difficulty of the second. This means your start is incredibly important—only students who do well on the first module get access to the higher-scoring second module.

Think of it like a video game where you have to beat the first level to unlock the more challenging (and higher-scoring) second level. If you don't do well in the first module, the second module will have an effective ceiling on your maximum possible score.

What This Means for Your Strategy

+ Starting strong is no longer just good advice, it's critical. Those first module questions are your gateway to a top score.

+ Familiarity with the digital interface is essential. Practice with the College Board's Bluebook app so nothing surprises you on test day.

+ The adaptive format can actually reduce test anxiety for some students. Your test will be more tailored to your level.

+ If you're aiming for top scores, you'll face the most challenging questions at the end, so preparation remains crucial.

How to Play the Game

This is where programs such as The Princeton Review excel. They don't waste time reteaching high school material. Instead, they teach you the actual rules of the game.

Rule 1: Use the Process of Elimination (POE)

First, eliminate the obviously wrong answers from multiple-choice questions. Often you can knock out two choices immediately. Then make an educated guess between what's left. Remember, you're only risking twenty-five cents to win a dollar!

Rule 2: Energy Management

Know when to skip questions and come back to them later, recognize when you're stuck in a sinkhole and move on, and prepare yourself to stay sharp through the entire test—get decent sleep, eat beforehand, and bring a protein snack.

Rule 3: Pattern Recognition

Spot recycled question types, learn the common answers that are easy traps to get caught in, and understand what each section is really testing. Give the test exactly what it wants—no more, no less.

Here's the truth: Rarely does anyone answer every SAT question correctly. (Although I did have one student who scored a perfect 1600 the first time!) That's not the point. The point is to maximize your score through smart strategy, just as Jeffrey learned in his DECA competition.

The PSAT Strategy: Elite Colleges' Early Alert System

Did you know that the PSAT can have more impact than a score of 1500 or higher on the regular SAT? That's because out of the 1.97 million (2024) high school juniors taking the PSAT, only 1% become National Merit Semifinalists. That list of 16,000 students is sent out nationwide before your senior year so that colleges can reach out to you.

Before I began pointing this out, Asian Americans who got over 1500 on their SAT didn't do so well on their PSAT—the more important test when you're a junior. They wouldn't prepare for it by at least taking practice PSAT tests, instead thinking, "Oh, it's not important, it's just the PSAT." So they'd be tricked, because it's shorter and seems easier (top scores are usually from 1490 to 1520). They'd fall into the PSAT trap of making careless mistakes.

Once I pointed out that the PSAT is key, I've routinely had at least one National Merit Semifinalist every year. In 2023, four of my juniors got the award, and all of them got into elite colleges. (Remember, though, that testing—and even becoming a NMSF—is only one part of the larger puzzle.)

The Bigger Picture

Remember this crucial truth: Your SAT score doesn't get you into college—it just makes you eligible. This is what I tell all my students. **You get eligible with your mind, but you get in with your heart.** And your heart is revealed in a story that makes people care about you.

Look at what happened in the University of California system. They didn't just drop the SAT requirement, they also limited AP classes to just two per year in GPA calculations (previously students could take unlimited APs to boost their GPA to astronomical levels). This double change dramatically impacted Asian American enrollment, which dropped from over 50% to around 30% at UC Berkeley, UCLA, and UC San Diego.

Why? Because many families had invested everything in the testing/AP strategy, missing the crucial truth about American college admissions—that test scores are just one piece of a much larger puzzle. The highest SAT score possible won't get you into an elite college if you don't have a compelling story to tell. Today the UC schools are looking at four essays that reveal your compassion, your ability to overcome and seek challenges, and your initiative and leadership in extracurriculars.

The Smart Way to Prepare

So what's the right way to approach SAT preparation? Here's my advice:

1. Don't spend your entire summer on test prep. That time could be better spent developing other aspects of your application that will make you unforgettable to admission readers, such as doing interesting volunteer work, taking part in competitive summer programs, researching a scientific or engineering problem, or performing in competitions.

2. Choose a test-prep program that understands the game. Look for one that focuses on teaching the rules and strategies, not just reviewing content you've already learned in school.

3. Remember that while the SAT rewards effort more directly than perhaps any other part of your application, it's still just one piece of the puzzle. Don't let it consume your entire junior year of high school.

4. Approach your SAT test the way Jeffrey approached his DECA competition. Once he stopped trying to run the perfect hotel and started focusing on what the simulation actually valued, everything changed. The same principle applies here.

5. For the digital SAT, make sure you practice with the actual Bluebook app from the College Board. The interface matters, and you need to be comfortable with the digital format.

6. Take the PSAT seriously. Prepare for it. It is definitely a superstar springboard.

Think of the SAT not as a test of your intelligence or an indication of your worth as a student, but rather as a game with specific rules, patterns, and strategies. Learn the rules. Practice the strategies. Play smart. But never forget that in the end, it's your compelling story—not just your test scores—that will set you apart.

KEY INSIGHTS:

+ The SAT is a game with specific rules. Learn to play it strategically rather than perfectly.

+ The PSAT is colleges' early alert system for superstars. Being among the 16,000 chosen from 1.97 million juniors puts you on elite colleges' radar.

+ Testing makes you eligible, but it's your story that gets you in.

CHAPTER 7

Talent and Passion— From Private Excellence to Public Impact

H ere's a quiz for you: Which of the following students do you think got into Rice University?

1. Alice: Level 10 piano certification, performed at Carnegie Hall, won multiple state competitions, had perfect grades and a 1550 SAT score.

2. Peter: Played clarinet in his school band, taught himself the French horn when the band needed one, created an iOS app to help his orchestra practice, grew a youth orchestra from seven to thirty members, performed in twelve different venues in the community.

3. Ma: Earned a black belt and won national championships in martial arts, had perfect grades, served as student body treasurer.

4. Advik: Had an advanced art portfolio, was a National Merit Semifinalist, earned perfect grades, and volunteered teaching art at senior centers.

The answer? Peter.

Surprised? After thirty years helping Asian and Indian American students get into elite colleges, I've discovered something crucial: Private excellence isn't enough anymore. All four of the students above had impressive achievements. But it was Peter who transformed his talent into something that made others care.

Let me share what I've learned about why some talented students get overlooked while others become truly unforgettable. It's not about how many certificates you have or what competitions you've won. It's what you do with your talent that counts.

Excellence in Isolation

Here's something I've noticed after working with talented students for so many years, particularly in the Asian American community: Many arrive in my office with impressive achievements like these:

— Piano certification at Level 10

— Black belts in martial arts

— Mastery of multiple instruments

— Advanced art portfolios

— Years of dance training

Yet something's missing. These accomplishments, impressive as they are, often remain private experiences—piano played only for the teacher, art seen only in class, martial arts practiced in the dojo but never shared. They're achievements accomplished in isolation, statistics without stories.

Let's be clear. If you're a concert-level pianist planning to study at Juilliard or an exceptional athlete being recruited for Stanford's team, your excellence alone might be enough. But for most students—even those who've achieved high levels in their particular arts or athletics—the path to standing out lies not just in what you can do but in how you use that to contribute to others.

Ask yourself these questions:

— What moments exploring your talent make you feel most alive?

— What needs in your community could your particular talent address?

— Could your talent solve problems in unexpected ways?

Excellence Through Contribution

Now let me share two stories that show different ways of transforming talent into contribution.

PETER: LEADERSHIP THROUGH MUSIC. I first met Peter when he was fourteen, and his only leadership experience was leading a team in his English class. He played trumpet, and when his school band needed a French horn player, he volunteered to learn that instrument. This might seem like a small detail, but it revealed something crucial: passion. When Peter told me this story, his eyes lit up. This, I realized, was what "set his hair on fire." Three key things emerged from his decision:

1. A senior student taught him to play the French horn, modeling kind and generous leadership by doing so.

2. This helped him to get into the selective Interlochen Center for the Arts summer program.

3. His mother realized his deep passion for music and gave him additional support.

As a result, his musical talent was transformed into leadership and contribution, and Peter

— became a drum major, leading his school band to win five out of six regional competitions;

— grew his youth orchestra from just seven members to thirty;

— performed at twelve venues and fundraisers for music education;

— later developed an iOS app connecting his newfound computer science interest with music; and

— got into Carnegie Mellon in computer science. In fact, when Peter was interviewed at Carnegie, his interviewer was most impressed with how he connected his love of computer science with music to make a difference for his orchestra.

DIVYA: CREATING COMMUNITY THROUGH DANCE.
Divya was an accomplished competitive dancer, but she wasn't planning to dance professionally. When she found her high school's dance club hidden in a dark corner with only two people signed up, she could have just focused on her private studio training. Instead, her mother's words became her motto: "Make your own world dance." What happened next shows the power of using talent to fill a need, as Divya

— built the dance club from two to more than one hundred members;

— created workshops in multiple dance styles;

— developed innovative teacher-student performances;

— made a home for students who didn't fit traditional molds; and

— got accepted at Vanderbilt University.

Transforming Passion into Contribution

Whether you've spent years mastering an instrument or are passionate about something completely unexpected, the following five principles can help you transform your interests into compelling contributions.

1. **Take private excellence public.** While Peter and Divya had traditional arts backgrounds, consider the less conventional example of Michelle, mentioned earlier in Chapter 2, who loved to crochet. Instead of keeping her hobby private, Michelle

   ✦ taught pregnant women at Stanford to knit baby blankets;

+ created connections between generations; and

+ built a sustainable volunteer program both in her high school and outside of it that continued after she graduated, crocheting and selling blankets to support unwed mothers.

The University of Chicago saw beyond the humble hobby of crocheting to recognize meaningful community building, and Michelle was accepted as a student. Knitting and crocheting constituted her primary extracurricular!

2. **Create what's missing.** Sometimes opportunity lies in what's absent. When Kevin realized his school had no tennis team, he

+ found a faculty champion;

+ built a network of support;

+ raised $5,000 for startup costs; and

+ created opportunities for future students.

Northwestern University recognized a student who saw a gap and filled it, and Kevin got in. And the boys' tennis team he started is still flourishing at his high school.

3. **Find the universal in your unique passion.** Here's where seemingly "uncool" or unusual interests can shine. Consider Amy, who was passionate about the Warrior Cats book series. Instead of hiding this interest, she

+ started writing fan fiction;

+ grew to manage a fan fiction website with 30,000 participants (which wasn't easy, since the "fans" often disagreed, so she had to learn conflict resolution among other things); and

+ applied her leadership skills to create "The Book Ocean" reading program in her high school so that a whole new generation could fall in love with Warrior Cats!

NYU saw beyond her unusual passion to recognize valuable leadership experience. Not only did she get into Stern School of Business, but she found her perfect major: human resources.

4. **Connect different worlds.** Although Ren was an accomplished violinist, he wasn't planning on a music career. Instead, he

   + discovered his love for music theory;

   + created free classes teaching pop song composition;

   + showed students how to use the mathematical patterns in hit songs to write their own; and

   + made complex theory accessible and fun.

He got into Dartmouth not because of his violin virtuosity, but because he bridged classical training with popular music through an accessible understanding of music theory—and brought that to his community.

5. **Scale up your impact.** Whatever your own starting point, look for ways to multiply your contribution. Think back to the students mentioned in this chapter as examples:

- Divya's dance club became a home for students who didn't fit in elsewhere, exponentially increasing the number of dancers in the club.

- Peter's youth orchestra membership tripled.

- Amy, the Warrior Cats fan, became a leader of thousands on her website.

- Kevin's tennis team created opportunities for future students and helped transform his school—the team even won regionals!

Finding a Path When You Think You Have No Talent

Here's something crucial to understand: You don't need a traditional talent or years of training to make a difference. Some of my most successful students started with these things:

— Interests others might consider trivial

— Hobbies they were almost embarrassed to mention

— Passions they thought weren't "impressive" enough

From Warrior Cats to crocheting, these students' hobbies helped them get into elite schools. Here's what's key:

— Start with whatever genuinely excites you.

— Look for ways to share that excitement.

— Find problems that you can solve.

— Create connections that others haven't made.

Once you've identified a promising idea to pursue, consider the following questions:

— What specific problem will you address?

— How will your talent provide a unique solution?

— Who could help you succeed? (Think mentors, peers, resources)

— How could your impact grow and continue after you graduate from high school?

The Challenge Factor

The most compelling stories often come from pushing beyond your comfort zone, taking risks, overcoming obstacles, or creating something new.

And here's what I left out about Kevin, who created the boys' tennis team for his high school: He was very shy, and the idea of starting a tennis team was intimidating. Yet he so wanted to play tennis for his school that he overrode his fear and got the support of the director of athletics. She helped pull his idea together to present to the school board. It was challenging for him to speak in front of twelve board members, but he wanted that tennis team.

Kevin felt totally deflated when the board said, "Sure, but you must raise $5,000 to prove you can make it viable." Until then he'd been the lone wolf, pursuing this on his own without the help of other students. But he took a chance and put up large posters around his school announcing that a boys' tennis team was starting and if students were interested, they should come to a kickoff meeting. Lo and behold, seventeen interested boys showed up, and together they raised the $5,000.

Kevin got into Northwestern, and ten years later his high school's varsity tennis team won the state title!

Making Your Choice: A Practical Guide

How might you make a contribution to your school or community? Start by asking yourself these questions:

1. What do I love doing, even if it seems unimpressive?

2. Who could benefit from what I know or care about?

3. What's missing in my community?

4. How could I bring different groups or interests together?

Then consider the following options:

For Traditional Arts/Athletics

If you've already invested years in piano, dance, martial arts, or sports:

— Look beyond personal achievement and find ways to share your knowledge—coach, teach, start a club.

— Create opportunities for others.

— Build communities around your skill, whatever it is.

For Unusual Interests

— Don't hide your passion.

— Look for unexpected applications.

— Find ways to lead or organize.

— Connect your particular interest to larger needs.

For Those Still Searching

— Pay attention to what naturally interests you.

— Notice problems you'd like to solve.

— Start small, but think about scaling up.

— Look for ways to connect people or ideas.

The Secret Sauce

The most successful college applications show these attributes:

— Genuine enthusiasm (What "sets your hair on fire"?)

— Initiative in sharing or developing that interest

— Creative problem-solving

— Lasting contribution

Colleges aren't just looking for the most accomplished pianist or the highest-ranked athlete. They're looking for students who use their own interests—traditional or unexpected, developed or emerging—to make a difference. What matters isn't whether your passion is "impressive" enough. It's what you do with it that counts.

KEY INSIGHTS:

+ Transform private excellence into public impact in order to stand out authentically.

+ Your passion doesn't need to be "impressive"— it needs to be challenging and make a difference.

+ Success comes from connecting what "sets your hair on fire" to larger needs, thus creating lasting change.

CHAPTER 8

Everybody's a Leader— They Just Don't Know It Yet

"I'm not student body president," Akira said quietly. "I'm not captain of any teams. How can I show leadership on my applications?"

I smiled, because Akira had already told me something remarkable. He had noticed that his school's computer club was dying; only three students still attended meetings. But instead of just letting it fade away, Akira had an idea. He wanted to transform it from a gaming club into a place where students could learn to code and create apps that helped their school.

"That," I told him, "is exactly what leadership looks like."

The Truth About Leadership

Let me share a secret learned from thirty years of helping Asian American students get into elite colleges: *Everyone's a leader—they just may not realize it yet.*

Before we explore different leadership styles, take a moment to recognize leadership that you're already showing. Ask yourself these questions:

— Did you explain something to help others understand?

— Did you notice a problem and try to fix it?

— Did someone come to you for help or advice?

— Did you make someone feel included?

— Did you organize something, even informally?

These moments matter. They show that leadership isn't about titles—it's about taking initiative to make things better.

Consider Andrew, a quiet Boy Scout who taught me something profound about leadership. When he first started as a Scout, he was the youngest kid in the room, desperately wanting to play dodgeball with the older Scouts. No one would let him join until one day, an older Scout said, "Here, take my spot." That simple act of inclusion changed everything for Andrew. From then on, he knew that leadership meant reaching out to the youngest in the room.

As he wrote in his Common App essay: "Now, whether I am a troop leader or camp counselor, I always look for that moment when I can give up my place to a younger Scout. Last summer, I had the chance to do so when we were playing soccer. Although I was dying to continue playing, I knew it was right to let some hungry kid take my place. I can only hope he passes it on and that he learned like I did, to always reach out to the youngest kid in the room."

Here's something crucial that most students (and many prep programs) don't understand: Leadership isn't about titles, nor is it defined by telling a group what to do. It's about seeing what's missing and having the initiative to fill that gap.

Think of it as the ancient Greeks did. They saw each person as a charioteer trying to control two powerful horses. One horse represents your desire to stay comfortable and safe. The other represents your drive to make a difference.

True leadership starts when you learn to guide these forces toward meaningful goals. It's not about being in charge—it's about being in motion toward something that matters.

Leadership That Colleges Notice

Leadership isn't about popularity or being recognized as someone who's in charge. It's about recognizing your own natural strengths and using them to make things better. Here are four natural leadership styles.

1. **The Pied Piper**

    + Naturally draws others to a cause

    + Builds enthusiasm and participation

    + Makes others want to join in

Example: Divya grew her school's dance club from two to one hundred members by creating an inclusive community.

2. **The Busy Bee**

    + Gets things done behind the scenes

- Creates systems and structures
- Makes projects sustainable

Example: Linda transformed her school's Speech & Debate Club by attracting new members and creating training materials and handbooks.

3. The Cheerleader

- Celebrates the success of others
- Builds team spirit
- Keeps motivation high

Example: Maya turned her ankle injury into an opportunity by becoming her badminton team's biggest supporter and strategist.

4. The Intuitive Leader

- Learns from personal experience
- Leads by example
- Transforms challenges into opportunities

Example: Andrew learned deeply what leadership was by the role modeling of other Boy Scouts.

Finding Your Natural Leadership Style

Take five minutes to reflect on the following:

1. **When working in groups, I usually**

   + get everyone excited about the project (Pied Piper);

   + make sure everything gets done (Busy Bee);

   + keep spirits high when things get tough (Cheerleader); or

   + share what I've learned through experience (Intuitive Leader).

2. **People often come to me when they need**

   + motivation to join something (Pied Piper);

   + help organizing or planning (Busy Bee);

   + support or encouragement (Cheerleader); or

   + advice based on experience (Intuitive Leader).

3. **I feel most energized when I'm**

   + getting others involved (Pied Piper);

   + creating systems that work (Busy Bee);

   + supporting team success (Cheerleader); or

   + sharing lessons learned (Intuitive Leader).

Circle your most common answers. This is likely your natural leadership style!

The Magic of Combining Styles

The most successful leaders learn to combine the styles above. Remember Akira? He started as a Busy Bee, creating coding tutorials and organizing meetings. Then he became a Pied Piper, attracting new members with exciting app projects. And finally he emerged as a Cheerleader, celebrating every new app his team created. The result? His computer club grew from three to thirty members, won second place in the Congressional App Challenge, and created three apps that continue to help their school community.

To create your own action plan for moving from following to leading, reflect on the following prompts:

1. **Start with observation.**

    + What bothers you at your school?

    + What could work better?

    + What problems do others ignore?

2. **Build your team.**

    + Find your champions (teachers, mentors).

    + Recruit passionate peers.

    + Create a support network.

3. **Take strategic action.**

    + Start small but think big.

    + Document your impact.

    + Build for sustainability.

The Leadership Secret Most Asian Students Miss

To be a leader, you don't need to

— be student body president;

— start a nonprofit;

— lead multiple clubs; or

— create massive fundraisers.

You just need to

— notice what's missing;

— take initiative to fill gaps;

— build a team to help; and

— create lasting impact.

Linda is a perfect example of this. As she says in her two-minute interview video for Pomona, "I have a 4.0 average, 1500 on my SATs, AND I am student body president, but that's not where I've really contributed to my school." She goes on to talk about how she helped her school's dying Speech & Debate Club to grow and become successful, so that by the time she graduated it was not only the largest club on campus but also the most successful, winning regional and state awards. Linda acknowledges that even getting elected to a school-wide position like Associated Student Body president wasn't as important as making a genuine difference by saving a dying club.

The Final Truth

The strongest leaders never work alone. Whether you're a Pied Piper inspiring others to join you, a Busy Bee making things happen behind the scenes, a Cheerleader keeping spirits high, or an Intuitive Leader sharing what you've learned, your contribution matters.

Leadership isn't about being in charge. It's about making things better. And that's something everyone can do, even if they don't know it yet.

Just ask Akira. His computer club isn't just about coding anymore—it's about creating positive change. Or consider Andrew, who learned that true leadership means noticing those who are left out and making them part of the group. Or think of Linda, who turned a struggling debate club into a thriving, successful community. That's leadership that sticks.

KEY INSIGHTS:

+ Everybody's a leader—they just may not know it yet.

+ Leadership isn't about titles; it's about seeing what's missing and taking the initiative to fill that gap.

+ The strongest leaders never work alone—they build teams to create sustainable change.

CHAPTER 9

Heart to Heart—Making Your Service Matter

*"If I look at the mass, I will never act.
If I look at one, I will."*
—Mother Teresa

Here's a mystery to consider: Why did Jackie get into USC with just 50 hours of service while Anna was rejected with 250 hours and three President's Volunteer Service Awards? The answer lies in what colleges really care about: not the hours you serve, but the hearts you touch. Let's look at their stories.

Anna meticulously logged her service, with 50 hours at food banks, 50 hours of beach cleanups, 75 hours at libraries, and 75 hours tutoring others. All of these hours were properly documented, earning her Gold President's Volunteer Service Awards. But they were all forgettable.

Jackie went on a 50-hour school trip to help build a house in Tijuana, while at home she did everything she could to fit in and not be noticed. But when she was working in Tijuana, she noticed a little boy, Chewy, who was being bullied by other boys. Her friends said she should leave him alone, that they were just visitors there. But Jackie reached out to him, and they sat together every day sharing her peanut butter sandwich by the house construction site. When her friends made fun of her—saying, "Jackie's got a boyfriend!"—she said, "Chewy is my friend." After that, even the bullies left him alone.

Here are the last two paragraphs of the college essay that got her into USC:

> On the last day I wanted to buy Chewy something special. I scooped him up and put him on my shoulders. I remember walking to the store in the glowing sunlight, my body feeling so filthy from the week of work and sweat, the ragged skyline of Tijuana behind us, and the weight of the happy little boy on my shoulders. When we got to the store, I dropped Chewy to the group and whispered to him, "*Usted puede comprar lo que quieres* (you can buy anything you want)." His little golden face lit up as he excitedly grabbed a warm orange Fanta. There seemed to be nothing else in the store but dusty shelves.

> On the day I left, Chewy ran beside our bus, tears mixing with the dirt on his face, yelling, "*No te vayas, no te vayas Yackie!*" I felt terrible and powerless and I hated my world as we drove off. But when I returned home, I had changed. I volunteered much more, worked to change the environment, and started my own company to give back. Chewy is forever running alongside my bus, calling "Yackie! Yackie!" I carry

him always on my shoulders. I say to him, "I will not take the easy way. I will speak up."

The difference? Jackie had an emotional, revelatory story that moved the admissions readers to want her. Anna had hours of service and many awards but made no emotional connection with her readers—in other words, she had no story.

Four Ways to Make Service Unforgettable

1. **Find your heart connection.** Instead of simply collecting hours, find what moves you. Like Albert, who

   + loved playing video games;

   + noticed that senior citizens were isolated after Covid and started teaching them to use iPads and play online games;

   + built a network of teen tech tutors;

   + created lasting connections between generations; and

   + got into UC Berkeley because he humanized technology.

2. **Transform the typical.** Don't just do what everyone else does—transform it! Like May, who

   + started as a regular volunteer in a small hospital, then noticed that young patients were bored and used her art skills to create a mobile art program;

   + trained other volunteers;

   + made the program sustainable; and

    ✦ got into UCLA because she'd fixed what was missing.

3. **Make one person's life better.** Alex was one of the first Asian American students that I worked with. He was a brilliant young mathematician, receiving both AMC and AIME math qualifications through high school, and was asked to join the UC Berkeley's prestigious Math Circle. Before the summer of his senior year, one of his teachers asked if he would tutor an eighth grader named Keith from East Palo Alto for part of the summer. His teacher told him that Keith was smart and needed to review Algebra 1 so he could take Algebra 2 in ninth grade. Alex was dubious, but he said yes because he liked the teacher. Twice a week all summer, he and Keith sat on a bench outdoors under a leafy tree and studied algebra.

In the essay that got Alex into Stanford he wrote:

When I first started tutoring Keith, I thought I was doing him a favor. But as the weeks went by, I realized he was teaching me as much as I was teaching him. One day we were studying the golden ratio, and out of the blue Keith said, "This ratio is related to the Fibonacci sequence, isn't it?" I almost fell off my chair. I hadn't thought of that. "How do you know about Fibonacci?" His face lit up with such joy that I thought, "Maybe I *will* be a teacher someday."

Alex got into Stanford not because he had tutored dozens of students but because he'd connected deeply with one of them, and he let that connection change him.

4. **Create lasting impact.** Like Kamal, who

+ started picking up trash at his local park and noticed that most of it was from takeout containers;

+ created a "Green Takeout" campaign;

+ got local restaurants to use eco-friendly packaging;

+ built a student team to continue the work; and

+ got into UC Davis's Environmental Science program.

Four Questions That Matter

Before starting any kind of service activity, ask yourself these questions:

1. Does this move my heart?

2. Can I make it better?

3. Will I connect deeply?

4. Can I create lasting change?

Service Traps

Here are two common traps to avoid:

The Numbers Game

Here's why collecting service hours like Pokémon cards just doesn't work:

— Everyone does it, so nothing stands out; like cancels like.

— You're left with no stories to tell.

— No hearts have been touched.

The Asian Tax Trap

Asian American students often fall into service pitfalls for these reasons:

— They think that more hours = better chances.

— They do what everyone else does and miss opportunities for innovation.

— They forget to make it personal by genuinely connecting with others.

A Quick Guide to Making Your Service Sticky

1. **Start with what you love.** Follow your passion, like the dancer who taught movement to senior citizens, the coder who created apps for educational non-profits, or the cook who started a cultural food bank.

2. **Look for what's missing.** Follow the example of Rachel, who volunteered at an animal shelter, noticed that Spanish-speaking families couldn't read pet adoption papers, created bilingual adoption materials, built a translation team, and transformed how the shelter served her community.

3. **Connect deeply.** Remember Jackie's words about Chewy: "I carry him always on my shoulders. I say to him, 'I will not take the easy way. I will speak up.'"

4. **Build for the future.** Make your service last by

creating systems, training others, documenting everything, and building partnerships.

Looking for your perfect service? Take out a piece of paper and write your answers to these questions:

— What makes me angry enough to want to change it?

— What skills do I have that could help others?

— What's missing in my community?

— Is there someone I could help consistently for a year?

Meaningful service isn't about collecting hours, checking boxes, and building résumés. It's about opening hearts— yours and those of others. It's about solving real problems and creating lasting change. And it's about making someone's life better.

Remember: You get eligible for college admission with your mind, but you get *in* with your heart. Your service journey is where that heart begins to beat for others.

KEY INSIGHTS:

✦ One deep connection beats a thousand shallow volunteer hours.

✦ Transform typical service into something remarkable.

✦ Create sustainable impact that will continue after you leave.

✦ Let your service change you as much as it changes others.

From Star to Superstar

A young scientist changed the way we think about stars. Until 1967, it was believed that stars just gradually faded away. But Jocelyn Bell Burnell noticed something different: a strange pattern in her data that others had missed. What she discovered became known as pulsars—stars that transform themselves into something remarkable through an intense process of change.

That's exactly what *you're* doing in this process! You've built your foundation as a star: strong grades, test scores, activities. But like Jocelyn Bell Burnell, you need to notice what others might miss—to see the gaps that need filling, to transform yourself from a star that simply shines into one that truly pulses.

The Gap Between Star and Superstar

Let me tell you about Mark. When I first met him, his parents were worried. While other Asian American students were racking up debate trophies and science fair awards, Mark spent hours playing MMORPGs (massive multiplayer online role-playing games). He had good grades (3.8 GPA) but no leadership positions, no prestigious awards—nothing that seemed to make him stand out.

But Mark noticed something everyone else had missed. In the complex online games he played, he was already a leader—coordinating raids of forty or more players, developing strategies, resolving conflicts between team members, and teaching newcomers how to succeed. Instead of hiding this "nontraditional" leadership, Mark decided to transform it by

— creating a summer coding camp and teaching underserved elementary kids how to create simple games;

— using gaming principles to make learning programming fun and accessible;

— building a team of high school volunteers to expand the program;

— documenting everything so that other schools could replicate it; and

— getting his gaming community to serve as online mentors.

UC Berkeley didn't admit Mark because he was a perfect student. They admitted him to their Computer Science program because he'd shown he could transform what seemed like an unproductive hobby into meaningful impact—teaching younger students while building a sustainable program that continued after he graduated.

The Art of Becoming Remarkable

Here's what Asian American students often miss: You don't need to win international competitions or cure cancer to be considered remarkable. Like a pulsar, you need to transform what you already have into something powerful enough to be noticed.

As Stanford puts it, they want "distinctive students who exhibit extraordinary impact outside the classroom." Notice that they don't just say "excellent students" or even "star students." They want something more—students who've transformed their talents into amazing impact. That's why Stanford is one of the most difficult schools to get into—of the 55,471 students who applied in 2025, only 2,190 got in (3.94%).

To move from star to superstar, it's important to exhibit these three qualities:

1. Initiative—see what's missing and take action.

2. Challenge—push beyond your comfort zone.

3. Compassion—connect with and help others.

In the pages ahead, you'll learn exactly how to do the following:

— Create something truly remarkable, even if you think you're "just ordinary."

— Tell your own story in an unforgettable way.

— Find colleges that value your unique story.

Every pulsar starts as a star. But successful stars are those that transform themselves—that notice what's missing and take initiative to fill those gaps. These are the ones who become truly unforgettable.

As Silicon Valley software pioneer Marc Andreessen says, "Be so good they can't ignore you. Make something." That's exactly what we're going to help you do: make something—and tell a story about it that can't be ignored.

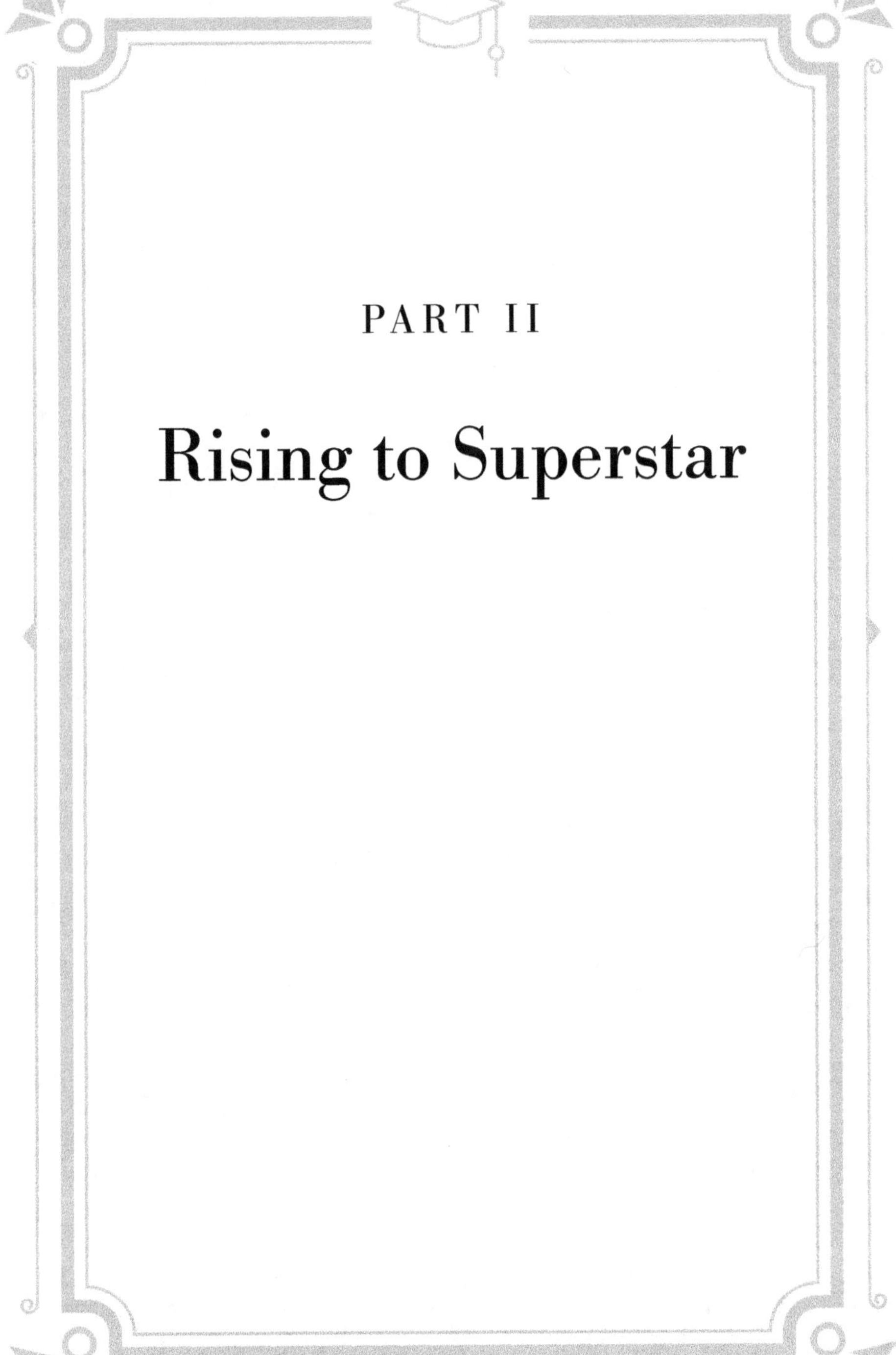

PART II

Rising to Superstar

CHAPTER 11

Your Remarkable Project– Creating Something Unforgettable

Doris Kearns Goodwin, the great presidential scholar, once said, "Whoever tells the best story gets to be president." Likewise, in college admissions, as the president of Reed College pointed out, "The storytellers get in." In elite colleges, however, the most compelling stories come from students who don't just achieve excellence—they create remarkable change.

Consider Adam's story. He couldn't focus on his AP History reading—not because the material wasn't interesting but because half the words in his textbook were literally crossed out. The margins were filled with years of student doodles, entire paragraphs highlighted into illegibility, and several key pages were missing entirely. "This is ridiculous," he muttered, looking around his classroom where other students were squinting at equally damaged books. "How are we supposed to learn like this?"

His initial plan was simple: organize a fundraiser to replace the worst of the books. But when he mentioned this to his AP History teacher, she sighed. "We've tried fundraisers before," she said. "The problem is bigger than you think. The whole school needs new books, not just our class."

Most students would have stopped there. A school-wide problem was too big for one high school junior to solve. But Adam remembered reading about David Lang's "Symphony for a Broken Orchestra"—how one student's concert had turned into a movement that repaired musical instruments across Philadelphia. So instead of giving up, Adam

— documented the scale of the problem, photographing damaged books across subjects;

— created "The School of Broken Books" campaign with a striking visual of a six-foot mountain of damaged textbooks in the school foyer;

— put on a theatrical performance of *Fahrenheit 451* with the damaged books used as props to fundraise within the community;

— got local media coverage that sparked community interest;

— built a coalition of parents, teachers, and local businesses; and

— launched a matching grant campaign with three local companies.

One year later, Adam stood on stage as the city mayor handed him an award—not just for raising over $9,452 to begin replacing textbooks across his school, but for creating a sustainable book maintenance and replacement program that would help students for years to come.

This is what a remarkable project looks like. It doesn't merely solve a problem—it transforms how things are done.

Why Remarkable Projects Matter

Here's what Stanford University says they're seeking: "Stanford looks for distinctive students who exhibit energy, personality, a sense of intellectual vitality and extraordinary impact outside the classroom." Note the key phrase "extraordinary impact." They're looking for not just achievement, not just leadership, but impact that transforms. They go on to explain, "The most compelling applicants for admission will be those who have thus far achieved state, regional, national, and international recognition in their academic and extracurricular areas of interest."[2]

Over the years I've had wonderful students who've achieved national and international recognition—a fifteen-year-old Olympic hurdler; an international badminton star; and one of my earliest students, Donna (who went to Yale and became a Rhodes Scholar), who helped map genomes. Others have won national fame as mathematicians, acing the AMC and AIME competitions.

Of course, not everyone can map genomes or go to the international level of math competitions, USAMO, so there must be other ways to go from ordinary to extraordinary.

---

2. The Princeton Review, *The Best 382 Colleges* (Princeton Review, 2017), Kindle edition, loc. 40055.

The Difference Between Good and Remarkable

First, let's be clear about something crucial: There's a fundamental difference between star-level activities and remarkable superstar-level projects.

Here are some examples of star-level activities:

— Starting a peer tutoring club at your school to help Algebra 2 students

— Organizing ten beach cleanups and receiving a certificate from a local environmental group

— Helping to lead a large fundraiser for a particular cause

— Reviving a dying club by rebuilding its reputation and numbers

And here are some superstar-level remarkable projects:

— With "Little Chopins," Cathy transformed individual piano lessons into a district-wide music education program serving underserved students across three schools, with ten trained instructors and sustainable funding raised through student performances.

— Peter turned his personal frustration with music practice tracking into an iOS app now used by youth orchestras across California to improve performance.

— Adam's "The School of Broken Books" campaign elevated a single classroom's need into a school-wide solution with lasting impact.

— Linda's Speech & Debate Club revolution didn't just revive a club, it created a comprehensive training system that took her team from zero to state champions.

The Difference? Scale, Innovation, and Lasting Impact

A remarkable project is important for those Asian Americans who don't face much adversity or challenge in their daily lives, because it shows adversity and difficulty over and beyond academics, athletics, and regular extracurriculars. In fact, the challenge is often at "collegiate level"—Peter with his iOS music app for his orchestra, Sam creating a tennis team for his high school, Linda taking over the Speech & Debate Club and running it like a class to win state championships, Dae leading middle schoolers' debate prep because no teacher wanted to take it on, and so on.

Peter (Carnegie Mellon University), Sam (Dartmouth University), Linda (Pomona College), and Dae (Stanford University) are all superstars. But you don't need to start out as a superstar to create a remarkable project. In fact, creating something remarkable can help transform you *into* a superstar. I'll help you uncover a remarkable project in your own life—in fact, it's likely already there! We just have to connect the dots and make it stronger.

The following are eight questions that have sparked remarkable projects from my students. Please answer them on a separate piece of paper.

1. **The principal question.** If you were principal of your school for a year, what would you do to change the school?

Don't just identify problems—imagine solutions. When Eliza saw her school's rundown appearance, she didn't just organize a cleanup. Inspired by Georgia O'Keeffe's words,

"I just want to make something beautiful," she created a sustainable campus beautification program that transformed her high school and continues to this day.

2. **The family impact question.** What challenges does your family face that others might share?

When Alice noticed her quadriplegic brother struggling with his communication device, she didn't just help him; she listened and observed so carefully that she was able to redesign the finger positioning mechanism. The solution she created is now used by others with similar challenges.

3. **The community gap question.** What's missing in your neighborhood?

Shaan didn't merely notice that his school district needed robotics resources, he helped build a coalition that created a facility serving five schools.

4. **The talent application question.** How could your skills solve problems in unexpected ways?

Mark transformed his gaming leadership experience into a coding education program. Remember: Remarkable projects often come from connecting different worlds.

5. **The service enhancement question.** How could existing programs work better?

Lawrence didn't just join his school's tutoring program—he created an online scheduling system that doubled participation, helping teachers, tutors, and students alike.

6. **The revival question.** What dying program could you transform?

Linda didn't only restart Speech & Debate Club; she created a comprehensive training system that took the team to the state championships.

7. **The next-level question.** How could you take what you love further?

Joanna and Jessica, twin sisters, loved reading so much that they didn't just start a book club. They created a district-wide literacy program connecting high school students with elementary readers.

8. **The personal growth question.** What challenge could help you grow?

Jonathan turned his lack of confidence into a remarkable project by going to Outward Bound and then creating an outdoor leadership program that helped build students' confidence across his district.

From Spark to Fire—How Small Ideas Grow

Remember: Remarkable projects may start small, but they can have a big impact. Here's how two students grew sparks into powerful changes.

Mark's Gaming Revolution

Initial spark:
"I coordinate forty-player raids online. Could these skills be used to teach others?"

Catching fire:
— Teaching five kids basic coding through gaming

— Using gaming strategies to make learning fun

— Creating simple, engaging tutorials

Spreading the flame:

— A team of gamers becoming instructors

— An after-school program taking shape

— Word spreading through the school

Full blaze:

— A program illuminating three district schools

— More than two hundred students learning coding

— Coverage by a local tech magazine

— "Gaming to Code" becoming a district model

— The program continuing to light the way for others

Jenny's Lunch Table Revolution

Initial spark:
"Why do international students eat alone?"

Catching fire:
— One table mixing languages

— Students sharing cultures over lunch

— Word spreading through ESL classes

Spreading the flame:
— A "lunch ambassadors" program starting

— Cultural celebration days beginning

— More tables joining in

Full blaze:
— The program lighting up the entire district

— ESL dropout rate falling by 17%

— Program featured in an education journal

— Six schools adopting the same model

— Creating lasting change

How to Make Your Own Project Remarkable

Want to make your own project remarkable? Then follow this path:

1. **Start with a spark.**

   + Notice what's missing or something that really bothers you about your school or community.

   + Ask "What if?"

   + Connect different worlds.

   + Find personal motivation.

2. **Fan the flames.**

   + Build a core team.

   + Find champions.

   + Test ideas on a small scale.

   + Document everything!

3. **Spread the fire.**

   + Create systems for growth.

   + Train others.

   + Build partnerships.

   + Make it sustainable.

4. **Leave a legacy.**

   + Create handbooks.

+ Establish plans to keep it going after you leave.

+ Build networks.

Essential Checklist for Remarkable Projects

You don't need to start with a huge idea. You need to start with something that matters to you—and with the determination to make it matter to others.

1. Notice something that's missing and figure out a way to supply it.

2. Gather a team to support you.

3. Find a champion to support you.

4. Document your success (with articles, videos, data).

5. Make your project sustainable by training others and creating systems.

As "The School of Broken Books" showed (page 79), even a frustrated student with a damaged textbook can create school-wide change!

In the next chapter, we'll explore how summer programs can become another pathway to doing something remarkable—transforming those precious weeks into opportunities.

KEY INSIGHTS:

✦ Remarkable projects don't just solve problems, they transform systems.

✦ Success comes from growing small ideas strategically.

✦ Lasting impact requires documentation, systems, and planning for continuity.

CHAPTER 12

Summer Programs— The Hidden Path to the Extraordinary

Here's a quandary for you: Why did Leo get into Duke University (less than 1% acceptance rate for Asian Americans) while Lily, with perfect grades and three prestigious summer programs, didn't? The answer lies not in what Leo did in class but in how he transformed his summer experience into something extraordinary.

Like the "remarkable project" discussed in the last chapter, the most compelling summer experiences don't just build your résumé—they transform you as a person, giving you

— material for unforgettable essays;

— champions for powerful recommendations;

— opportunities for remarkable projects; and

— a progression that shows genuine intellectual growth.

Let's see how three very different approaches created transformative stories.

From Experience to Transformation

Whether she was creating rainbow cabbage through water chromatography or extracting strawberry DNA in the eighth grade, Mai's favorite subject had always been science. Like every other student during the pandemic, however, she was stuck doing artificial labs through a computer screen. When summer came, she was determined to find real lab experience.

The rejections hit hard. COSMOS (California State Summer School for Math and Science) said no. So did ASDRP (Aspiring Scholars Directed Research Program). Each "no" cut deeper, until the last rejection made her feel like a failure. But Mai had a rule: "You can be sad for one day. Tomorrow, we get back up."

So she did something remarkable. She started sending cold emails to professors at Stanford—one after another, ten in total. When a professor in a Stanford cancer lab offered her a chance to work on brain tumor research—especially meaningful, since she'd lost her favorite aunt to cancer—she ran through her house hugging her mother. "I can do lab research!"

But here's what transformed a lucky break into something remarkable: The lab probably didn't expect much from a fifteen-year-old, but Mai was determined. Months before her internship began, she

— studied peer-reviewed papers about brain tumors during her lunchtime;

— watched PCR (polymerase chain reaction) technique videos during her commute;

— visualized experiments before going to bed; and

— researched lab protocols until her computer crashed from too many open tabs.

By her second week, in stark contrast to the one PCR she'd gotten to do in class, Mai was running five hundred PCR reactions daily. Her mentor said she was "better than some graduate students." But Mai wasn't done. The next summer, when she was allowed to pursue an independent project, she discovered a potential way to slow tumor growth. This work won her the American Academy of Neurology Neuroscience Research Prize for undergraduates. Standing at the podium in Seattle, this high school student who'd barely been in a lab before thought, "You ain't seen nothing yet!"

A Different Path— From Samosas to Breakthrough

While Mai created her opportunity through sheer determination, Kamal's journey began differently—with a simple recipe and a basic chemistry class. When he first joined ASDRP's (Aspiring Scholars Directed Research Program) computational chemistry program, he could barely understand the protocols. It reminded him of his grandmother's samosa recipe, where the first instruction simply said "knead until smooth," as if that explained the delicate balance needed for perfect dough.

"From the moment I stepped into the lab," Kamal wrote, "I knew this wasn't going to be like high school chemistry. But my grandmother always said, 'To make perfect samosas, you must first learn patience with each fold.'"

Like his early attempts at samosas that produced nothing but torn wrappers and lumpy filling, his first weeks were filled with errors—wrong measurements, contaminated samples, misunderstood procedures. But instead of hiding his failures, Kamal did something different: He documented every mistake and solution, creating detailed notes in the margins of his protocols, just as he had done with his grandmother's recipe.

By his second summer, something remarkable happened. The student who once couldn't understand basic procedures was now leading a research team. When new students joined his project, instead of just giving them protocols to follow, he remembered his grandmother's wisdom: "My first hundred samosas were disasters too, beta. If you want to master anything, you must make your first ninety-nine mistakes."

This approach transformed not just his team's results, but how the lab approached research. Under his leadership

— the team expanded their computational project to include experimental validation;

— they developed new ways to visualize molecular interactions;

— they created a training system that continued after he graduated; and

— most importantly, they discovered a novel approach to protein binding that caught the attention of senior researchers.

When Kamal was chosen as one of twelve Clark Scholars nationally, the selection committee noted not just his research achievements, but how he had transformed the learning process itself. "Sometimes," Kamal wrote in his application essay, "you have to make ninety-nine mistakes before you can create something tasty."

The Searcher of Hidden Light— Trulee's Story

> "I'm staring into what looks like ordinary seawater when suddenly the entire dish explodes into blue fire. Tiny stars cascade through the darkness, each pinprick of light a living creature no bigger than a grain of sand. I've never seen anything so beautiful in my life, and I'm crying before I realize it."

This was Day 18 in Trulee's transformation from English major to scientist. While Mai fought for her opportunity and Kamal built his expertise step by step, Trulee found her remarkable moment in an unexpected place. As an English major who spent her days analyzing metaphors in modern novels, she had only taken one science class when her mother's college friend offered her a chance to do summer work in UC Santa Barbara's marine biology station.

At first, she was relegated to washing glassware and organizing sample jars. "For weeks," she wrote, "the researchers spoke in a language I couldn't understand—talking about dinoflagellates and luciferin like they were discussing old friends. I felt like I was reading a book written in code."

But everything changed the night Dr. Martinez asked her to stay late to help with a special experiment. They were studying bioluminescent plankton—microscopic organisms that create their own light when disturbed. In a darkened lab lit only by red lights, Trulee watched as the scientist gently swirled a petri dish of what looked like ordinary seawater.

The reaction was instantaneous and magical. Thousands of tiny blue lights erupted across the surface, like someone had scattered liquid starlight. Each disturbance created new constellations, new galaxies of living light that pulsed and swirled before fading back to darkness.

"It's a defense mechanism," Dr. Martinez explained, as Trulee stood transfixed. "When they sense danger, they light up to startle predators. It's a last-ditch effort to survive."

But Trulee heard something else entirely. Here were creatures so small they were invisible to the naked eye, yet when threatened, they chose to burn brightly rather than disappear quietly. It was the most beautiful metaphor she'd ever encountered— not written on a page, but alive and glowing in her hands.

That summer transformed her path, and she went from

— analyzing literary metaphors to discovering living ones;

— reading about heroic characters to studying heroic organisms;

— writing about imaginary worlds to exploring real ones; and

— loving fictional light to creating actual illumination.

"Even now, two years later," she wrote, "I can still see those first pinpricks of bioluminescent light behind my eyelids. But this time, it's not Dr. Martinez explaining the science to me—it's me explaining it to the next curious English major who thinks science isn't for them."

Trulee was moved by the defense mechanism in these tiny creatures who chose to "burn brightly rather than disappear quietly" when threatened. It's a metaphor any English major would fall in love with, because it connects to courage, visibility, and choosing to shine despite danger. It's literally about finding light in darkness, which works on multiple levels for someone, like Trulee, discovering her path.

A Practical Guide to Finding Your Own Summer Path

After seeing how Mai, Kamal, and Trulee transformed their summers, you might be wondering, "Where do I even start?" Let me share the three surprisingly simple steps you can take.

1. **Use a simple search to find programs.** Here's a secret that expensive college consultants don't tell you: Start by Googling or use Perplexity (AI research app). Here are a few ideas of what to search for:

   + Best high school summer programs for engineering

   + Best high school summer premed programs

   + Top business summer programs for high school students

   + Best summer writing programs for high school students

Read multiple lists and look for programs that appear consistently. But remember: As Mai showed us, sometimes the best opportunities aren't on any list.

2. **Understand program levels.** Just as Kamal built his way from ASDRP to Clark Scholar, you need to know where to start. Do research on programs such as the following:

   + "Reach" programs (5–10% acceptance rates): SIMR (Stanford Institutes of Medicine Summer Research Program), ASDRP summer session, RSI (Research Science Institute, MIT), Clark Scholars

   + "Target" programs (25% acceptance rates): COSMOS, KP Launch, UCLA Precollege Science and Engineering

   + "Foundation" programs (50% or higher acceptance rates): local college labs, ATDP (UC summer course program for ninth and tenth graders), research programs like Lumiere or Polygence where you work with a mentor to research a STEM issue, John Hopkins Center for Talented Youth (CTY)

Don't be afraid to start at the Foundation level. Remember: Trulee had only taken one science class before her Stanford internship. What matters isn't where you start, but how you transform the experience.

3. **Create your strategy.** Like the three students just described, you need to have both a plan and flexibility.

If nothing has worked yet (the Mai strategy),

— research professors in your field at a local university;

— craft thoughtful emails to them;

— prepare extensively to be ready when opportunities come; and

— use rejections as motivation.

If you're building up (the Kamal strategy),

— start with Foundation-level programs—Lumiere, ASDRP early acceptance (75% acceptance rate), Polygence, precollege programs;

— document everything;

— look for ways to improve systems; and

— create resources for others.

If you're bridging separate fields (the Trulee strategy),

— use your own unique perspective to connect different disciplines;

— find gaps that you can fill; and

— create new understanding for others, like Trulee did for students interested in humanities and science research.

Summer Programs—Another Path to Remarkable

Summer programs offer a different approach to creating something remarkable. Instead of building from scratch, you can transform existing opportunities into something extraordinary. Here are three ways to make programs remarkable.

1. **Transform how things are done.** Just as some students create remarkable projects by filling in the gaps, you can make existing programs better, like Kamal did.

   + Notice what's missing in the current training.

   + Suggest better ways to do things.

   + Create systems that will help others learn.

   + Build resources that will last after you're gone.

Kamal didn't just learn computational chemistry. He transformed how his lab trained new students—using his grandmother's samosa wisdom to create a new approach.

2. **Connect what's disconnected.** Instead of creating something completely new, bridge existing worlds, like Trulee did.

   + Bring perspectives from one field to another.

   + Find connections that others miss.

   + Use your own unique background as an advantage.

   + Create unexpected combinations.

Trulee didn't invent scientific research or literary analysis, but she brought them together in a way that made both of them richer.

3. **Push beyond boundaries.** When existing programs say "no," find a new path, like Mai did.

   + Create your own opportunities.

+ Prepare so thoroughly that you can't be ignored.

+ Transform rejections into stepping stones.

+ Make your own path remarkable.

When Mai's mentor at the lab complimented her on her lab skills, she smiled to herself. If her mentor only knew that everything Mai knew was learned via YouTube! But it had worked, because Mai had been willing to devote hours before her internship learning those skills.

The Practical Path—Making It Happen

While Mai, Kamal, and Trulee showed us what's possible, let's talk about what comes after you do your Google or Perplexity search.

Step 1: Strategic program selection

— Research programs that match your current level of knowledge and experience

— Create a spreadsheet with these three categories:

+ Reach (like SIMR for research or Wharton for business)

+ Target (like COSMOS, Babson)

+ Foundation (local programs, school initiatives, NSLC (National Student Leadership Conference))

Step 2: Track essential details for each program

— Application opening and closing dates

— Essay requirements

— Recommendations required

— Program dates

— Cost and financial aid options

Some Top Programs to Consider

Many successful students start with one of the following summer programs when they are in high school:

— ASDRP (Aspiring Scholars Directed Research Program) in Fremont, CA

— COSMOS mathematics and science program for California students, at several state campuses

— KP Launch (Kaiser Permanente internship program)

— Lawrence Berkeley National Laboratory high school internship program

— Northwestern University's Medill Cherubs journalism program

— University of Pennsylvania Coding Academy

— Babson College or Haas School of Business (B-BAY at University of California) business programs

— Polygence, Lumiere, or Horizon Halo research programs

— HSHSP (Michigan State's high school honors program in science, math, and engineering)

— Engineering Summer Program (ESP) at the University of Wisconsin-Madison

Your Summer Program Essay

What makes a compelling summer program essay? Let's look at three different approaches.

1. **STEM programs (COSMOS example):** "Tell us about your interest in science, technology, engineering, or mathematics. What experiences have contributed to your interest? What do you hope to learn or experience at COSMOS?" (750 words)

   In your essay, show your

   + genuine curiosity and readiness to learn;

   + connection between your past experiences and the program goals; and

   + vision for using this opportunity.

   For an example of Alice's winning COSMOS essay, see Appendix 3 (page 315).

2. **Research programs (ASDRP example):** "Describe your research interests and what motivates you to pursue research in your area of interest." (500 words)

   In your essay, demonstrate your

   + initiative and eagerness to learn;

   + understanding of the research process; and

   + interest in collaboration.

   For an example of Vivek's winning ASDRP essay, see Appendix 3 (page 317).

3. **Journalism programs (Medill Cherubs example):**

"Why are you interested in the Medill Cherubs Summer Program?" (300 words)

In your essay, highlight your

- passion for journalism;

- eagerness for hands-on learning;

- future aspirations in the field; and

- desire to engage with peer journalists.

Hidden Opportunity to Build Your Champion

Here's something crucial that most students miss: Summer programs aren't just about the experience—they're your chance to develop a strong recommendation for your college applications. Start early.

— Find teachers in subjects related to your interests.

— Share your goals and aspirations with them.

— Ask thoughtful questions about their field.

— Keep them updated on your progress.

— When you move on to another class, stay in touch.

Remember: The strongest recommendations come from teachers who've watched you grow.

Making Your Summer Remarkable: Four Keys

1. **Start with documentation.**

   - Keep detailed notes (like Kamal's recipe and science notes, page 93).

+ Record your failures and your solutions.

+ Save everything—you're building a story!

2. **Look for gaps.**

   + What's missing in the program?

   + What could work better?

   + Where could your unique perspective help?

3. **Build for others.**

   + Create training materials.

   + Help develop better systems.

   + Make your impact sustainable.

4. **Transform the experience.**

   + Don't just learn—innovate.

   + Don't just achieve—improve.

   + Don't just participate—transform.

The strongest summer programs aren't just about what you gain; they're about what you leave behind. Whether it's Mai's new training approach, Kamal's lab protocols, or Trulee's bridge between humanities and science, remarkable summers create lasting change.

Summer Program Checklist

1. Become so good that you can't be ignored!

2. Pick programs that fit where you are in your development in STEM, business, etc. Getting into top

summer programs is progressive—you work your way up from Foundation level to Target and then Reach.

3. Pick a range of programs—Reaches, Targets, and Foundations—and put them on spreadsheet.

4. Spend time writing an excellent essay. Use the summer program models in Appendix 3.

5. Get an excellent recommendation—talk to your teacher about the program and give him/her your résumé.

6. Apply for early application if possible (e.g., there's a 3% acceptance rate to get into ASDRP for the summer session, but if you do early application, it's a 75% acceptance rate!).[3]

---

3. Aspiring Scholars Directed Research Program, "Application Statistics and Early Application Benefits," ASDRP Official Website, accessed December 2024, https://www.asdrp.org.

CHAPTER 13

The Pathway to Sticky Essays

After exploring how to create a remarkable project and participating in transformative summer programs, you arrive at perhaps the most critical element of your college application: the essay. By now you're becoming someone who cannot be ignored, and your experiences aren't just impressive achievements to list on your application—they're the foundation for essays that truly "stick" with admissions officers.

A "sticky essay" is one that makes your unique qualities and potential become impossible to overlook or forget. Remember this crucial truth: **The story in your essay is what gets you into college.**

The remarkable things you've done provide the raw material, but the essay is where you transform those experiences into a compelling narrative that makes admissions officers fight for you in the committee room. Each student featured in the previous chapters didn't just do something impressive—they learned how to articulate their journey, insights, and growth in ways that made their applications unforgettable.

Standing on the Shoulders of Superstars

Here's something crucial to understand as you transition into writing your essays: **You will not be starting from scratch.** One of my most valuable offerings from thirty years of college admissions coaching is my extensive collection of essay models that have helped students gain admission to elite universities.

When a student comes to me with their story, I sometimes say, "This reminds me of how John or Tresaida approached it," and I rummage through my files to find a model for them. You're about to receive the fruit of my decades of experience—a treasure trove of sticky essay models to learn from.

As T.S. Eliot wisely noted, "Immature poets imitate; mature poets steal; bad poets deface what they take, and good poets make it into something better, or at least something different." In the next chapter, you'll see this principle in action.

— Andy used "The Chewy Effect" as a template for his essay about volunteering at a Montana Indian reservation, based on Jackie's approach (page 64-65), helping him gain admission to Washington University in St. Louis.

— Jade modeled an opening line from Jack's essay (page 117)—"To understand where I am coming from as a student and musician, I must first tell you two secrets"—and made it her own.

— Some students followed Kamal's focused and patient path to becoming a superstar through summer programs like Clark Scholars and ASDRP (page 93), leading to acceptances at Johns Hopkins, Carnegie Mellon, and other elite institutions.

— Other students learned from the way Kabir did his Golden 20 courses—taking some of them outside of his regular high school courses (page 32). Your high school may not put outside courses on your transcript, but you can add them to your application as Kabir did and send transcripts to colleges, and they'll factor them in.

Remember: **Superstars borrow from other superstars.** The students featured in this book have generously allowed me to share their essays so that you can study them, extract the elements that resonate with you, and craft something uniquely your own.

As American author Tony Robbins believed about modeling success, why spend years figuring out what works when you can learn from those who have already mastered the path?

CHAPTER 14

The Sticky Essay—
Storytellers Get In

"What sticks is what matters."

—Zhaoping Li

*"The world is already full of marketers
and businessmen. The world doesn't need more of that.
The world needs healers and problem-solvers who
use their hearts. Your heart is a million times
more powerful than your brain."*

—J. Jarre

Now let's explore how to craft essays that stick, using as your foundation both the remarkable experiences you've cultivated and the proven models I'm about to share. This chapter will guide you through the process of turning your standout achievements into standout essays that no admissions officer can ignore.

The Power of Story over Essay

Here's a quiz for you: What's the best way to get someone on the same page as you are?

A. Tell them a story

B. Pay them a compliment

C. Make them laugh

D. Say something surprising

If you chose A, you're already thinking like a successful college applicant. Here's the bottom line: To get into a great college, you're not going to write an essay. You're going to tell a story. Remember, as the president of Reed College famously said, "The storytellers get in."

Why is this true? It's because we're hardwired for stories. Give us a beginning, a middle, and a payoff, and we're hooked. Consider this joke:

Two cows were talking in the field. One said, "Have you heard about the mad cow disease that's going around?"

"Yeah," the other cow says. "Makes me glad I'm a penguin."

Or this one:

A young boy enters a barbershop, and the barber whispers to his customer, "This is the dumbest kid in the world. Watch while I prove it to you." The barber puts a dollar bill in one hand and two quarters in the other, then calls the boy over and asks, "Which do you want, son?" The boy takes the quarters and leaves.

"What did I tell you?" said the barber. "That kid never learns!"

Later, when the customer leaves, he sees the same boy coming out of the ice cream store. "Hey, son! May I ask you a question? Why did you take the quarters instead of the dollar bill?"

The boy licks his cone and replies, "Because the day I take the dollar, the game is over!"

The payoff is what makes these stories memorable—they stick with you. That's exactly what your college essay needs to do: make admissions officers remember you after reading thousands of applications.

Your Fifteen Minutes of Fame

None of my rising seniors last June knew how to tell an irresistible story. But they learned, and so will you. My twelve seniors got into Carnegie Mellon, Columbia, Cornell, Duke, Emory, Johns Hopkins, Rice, Stanford, UCLA, UC Berkeley, UC San Diego (UCSD), and the University of Texas at Austin.

What you might not realize is how the college admissions process actually works. You probably imagine a group of admissions officers poring over your application with great interest and care, saying, "Wow, this is wonderful!" and "Listen to this!" as they read parts of your essay aloud to each other.

The reality? You get about fifteen minutes of fame. Two admissions officers look at your application for approximately fifteen minutes each. That's it. In those precious minutes, you need to make an impression so powerful that they champion your admission.

Consider these staggering numbers: In 2023, Stanford received 45,227 applications for 2,349 available places (a 4.1% acceptance rate). This means that out of every one hundred people who applied, fewer than four got in. UCLA, on the other hand, had 149,000 applications for 12,844 places (a 8.6% acceptance rate).[4] Your competition is fierce—which is why your story must be one that sticks.

The Asian Quota Challenge

An additional challenge for many applicants is what I call the "Asian Tax," or quota. Despite what colleges say, you are often admitted according to your demographic—Blacks compete against Blacks, whites compete against whites, and Asians compete against Asians. This quota ranges from a high of 40% of eligible Asians admitted to Caltech to only 8.1% admitted to Harvard—the average admitted during a twenty-year period ending in 2017.[5] This 8.1% Harvard average only changed when a lawsuit was filed by Students for Fair Admissions alleging that Harvard discriminated against Asian Americans applicants, rating them lower on subjective measures and imposing a "soft quota" or engaging in "racial balancing." This is despite the fact that these Asian applicants scored highest on objective measures like test scores, grades, and extracurricular activities (see Appendix 1).

Before the SAT was dropped at UC schools (2021), Asians made up 41% of *accepted applicants* at UC Berkeley, 50% at UCSD, and 39% at UCLA, while Latinos were 25% UC-wide.

---

4. Stanford University, "Undergraduate Admission Facts 2023," Stanford University Office of Undergraduate Admission, 2023; University of California, Los Angeles, "UCLA Admissions Statistics 2023," UCLA Undergraduate Admission, 2023.

5. Students for Fair Admissions, Inc. v. President and Fellows of Harvard College, Trial Exhibit P001 (2018); California Institute of Technology, "Undergraduate Admission Statistics," Caltech Office of Undergraduate Admissions, accessed December 2024.

Since the SAT/ACT was eliminated, in 2025 Asians got in 34% on average UC-wide, Latinos at 36%, and whites at 21%. To put that in context, Asians make up 17% of California's population, while Latinos are 38%.[6]

This demographic competition means that excellent Asian students can cancel each other out, especially when combined with stereotyping. Admissions officers may think, "Oh sure, most Asian Americans are good in math, they play a musical instrument, play badminton, and want to major in STEM or business." They see Asians as good but somewhat boring students who are "AP machines," often serve as secretaries and treasurers of clubs, and earn President's Volunteer Service Awards.

The good news is that I'll show you how to break through this stereotyping and use your fifteen minutes of application attention successfully in ways that other applicants don't.

A Tale of Two Applicants

Let's examine a revealing case study. Two students applied to Columbia University. One got in and one didn't. You choose which one was accepted.

Student A: Maya

— Wanted to be a doctor

— Completed a eight-week competitive internship at Alta Bates Summit Medical Center

— Had a 4.0+ GPA, 1540 SAT score

---

6. University of California, "UC Admissions by the Numbers," UC Office of the President, 2021–2025; California Department of Finance, "California Population Demographics," accessed December 2024.

— National Merit Semifinalist

— Accomplished violinist with regional competition awards

— Volunteered at local children's hospital

— Vice President of Premed Club

— Strong recommendations

— Submitted recording of her violin performance to Columbia

Student B: Jack

— Wanted to be a businessman

— Had a 3.1 overall GPA (raised to 4.0 in his final two semesters) and 1480/1540 SATs

— Ran cross-country

— Spent two weeks at Haas Business School in a competitive program and won an award

— Worked as a DJ, making good money

The obvious choice seems to be Maya—a National Merit Semifinalist and an award-winning violinist with a prestigious Alta Bates internship. She appears to have much more going for her than Jack does—an absolute superstar! But now let's read excerpts from their essays.

Maya's Essay: Academic Challenge

"Vitals are stable," the nurse announced as I watched the surgical team work. Standing in the observation area of Alta Bates's cardiac unit, I felt privileged to witness a complex heart procedure. This was exactly what I had hoped for when I applied to their competitive summer internship program.

I was selected as one of twelve students from over 2,000 applicants for the Alta Bates Medical Exploration Program. During my eight weeks there, I was determined to maximize every learning opportunity. I even created a detailed schedule to shadow physicians across multiple departments.

Through careful planning and persistence, I managed to observe procedures in cardiology, oncology, pediatrics, and emergency medicine. I watched surgeons perform intricate operations, observed radiologists interpret complex scans, and learned diagnostic techniques from experienced physicians. In the pathology lab, I examined tissue samples and learned to identify cellular abnormalities.

One memorable day, I spent twelve hours in the emergency department, observing how doctors handled everything from minor injuries to life-threatening trauma. The fast-paced environment taught me about medical decision-making under pressure.

By the end of my internship, I had logged over two hundred hours of clinical observation and completed an independent research project on patient care protocols. My supervisor commended my dedication and attention to detail.

This experience confirmed my commitment to pursuing medicine. I now understand the complexity and responsibility that comes with being a physician. Because of this comprehensive internship, I am more determined than ever to become a doctor and contribute to healthcare.

Jack's Essay: Personal Challenge

To understand the world that I come from and how it shapes my dreams and aspirations, I must first tell you an incident that happened when I was fifteen.

Staring out the window of the restaurant, I noticed a homeless man. I figured he was in his late sixties because he was bald, skinny, and trembled as he walked. As the man shambled past, my mother suddenly jumped up and ran outside. She rushed up to the man, he smiled, and they spoke for a short time. He, along with my mom, walked back into the restaurant and sat down. It made me proud to see my mom being so generous to this homeless stranger.

After sitting down, she looked into my eyes and said something that I will never forget. "Jack, say hello to your father."

I had not seen my father for years. There had been times that I thought about him and what I would tell him if I ever saw him again, but when I saw him sitting across from me in the restaurant that day, I did not know what to say.

The next time I saw my father he was lying in a casket.

Jack's essay continues, describing how his father's death from AIDS and drug addiction affected him, his own struggles at an elite high school among affluent peers who were much more academically prepared, his taking on DJ work to help his mother financially, and eventually finding his way academically. He concludes, "My father had given up before he died. I will not."

The Power of a Sticky Essay

Who got into Columbia? Jack did—with a 3.1 GPA and his biggest accomplishment being a successful DJ stint and helping his mother financially!

Why? First, he had a compelling story—beginning with the shocking revelation that the homeless man was his father, proceeding to his father's death from AIDS, and explaining his academic struggles. Finally, he sets up a problem: How is this kid going to overcome all this and get into an Ivy League school? And he had the perfect payoff: "My father had given up before he died. I will not."

Jack was a storyteller. His narrative made us care about him. It's about a conflict—a problem he needed to solve. It had a great payoff that made it sticky, meaning that it elicited an emotional response from the reader.

Maya's essay, while well written and showing initiative, lacked

— personal vulnerability or character revelation;

— a meaningful problem to solve;

— emotional connection;

— an inspiring insight or transformation; and

— a memorable payoff.

It reads like a competent report rather than a story that makes us care about Maya as a person. But Jack's essay surprises us, makes us immediately feel something, and has a beautiful payoff. His commitment at the end sticks with the reader.

Stories get people to act. They inspire energy and action. For college applications, your story should inspire the admissions officer to let you in, to accept you. That's exactly what happened to Jack.

In addition, before sending in his Early Decision application, Jack made sure his story reached his high school recommenders (who, like most teachers, only knew him from class). They and his high school counselor wrote sticky recommendations that backed up his amazing transformation. In two semesters, once motivated, Jack went from a 3.1 GPA to a 4.0 in difficult AP courses, and he raised his 1480 SAT score to 1540 in the end. Clearly, this student showed enormous potential—and Columbia saw it.

This is why it's important to write a draft of your main essay over the summer before your senior year, so that you can share it with your recommenders in early fall. They can then reinforce what you're saying in your story.

The Secrets of Storytelling

Now that you understand why storytelling is crucial for your college application, I'm going to share the secrets of how to become a good storyteller and write a terrific college essay. Then I'll take you through an exercise—Digging for Diamonds—that will you help you find your own irresistible story. Let's start with the eight secrets of sticky essays.

Secret 1: Become a good storyteller. You already know this first secret—you're not going to write a college essay at all! You're going to tell a story about your life.

Secret 2: You only have fifteen minutes of fame. Use your time wisely by making your story sticky. When that admissions officer reads your essay in their fifteen-minute review, a sticky essay will resonate and be memorable. Think about how commercials and pop songs try to be catchy so you can't get them out of your head. That's what you want your essay to do—stick in the mind of the admissions officer.

I can't tell you how many times my students receive acceptance letters that specifically mention their essays. Once a college president actually wrote by hand on the admissions letter itself, "Congratulations! Your essay was so moving!"

Secret 3: The "Asian Tax" or quota is real. We've discussed this challenge already. The key is to use your essay to transcend stereotypes and showcase your unique qualities.

Secret 4: You only need one sticky essay. You just need an essay that positions you to stand out among other students. In your fifteen minutes of fame, you need to make it sticky or your application will slide right into the reject file. And don't worry about the prompts that are given—just write about something that's important to you in a way that shows conflict (problem-solution).

Aristotle, in his *Poetics*, describes a well-told story as "the tying and untying of the knot." You start your essay with the knot (the problem), and the rest of the essay is the untying of that knot (the solution).

Maya didn't solve a problem; she just described her internship. But Kamal did—he'd been rejected from all his summer programs because of his lack of experience. In his essay, he solved that problem well enough that he discovered something scientific. Jack also solved a problem—overcoming his father's death and his own academic struggles to earn his way into Columbia.

Secret 5: Dig for diamonds in your own life. It's easier to write a compelling essay than you think, as long as you approach it systematically. Every student has a story—you just need to find yours.

Secret 6: Treat yourself as two people—the writer self and the editor self. The reason for this approach is that you want to write your first drafts with your heart, not your critical brain.

Maya's essay is a good example of that; she wrote from her brain, not her heart. The writer self just writes—no judgment, just get your stories out. Your writer self needs a chance to say its piece without someone—particularly that critic in your head—saying, "Are you sure? This seems kind of dumb. Not very sticky." Instead, just let the words flow.

Secret 7: When you're in the mood, finish writing the damn thing! Once you've found your story and you're feeling inspired, keep going until you've completed a draft. Don't interrupt the creative flow.

Secret 8: Don't kill your babies. Don't show your essays to anyone too early in the process. Your parents will ask, and you can tell them about your work, but don't have anyone read your early drafts. They'll criticize them, try to change things, question your topic choices, or redirect you.

It's too early for feedback. You just want to write and write and see what develops without anyone peeking over your shoulder to see if it's done. Ernest Hemingway said it well: "I don't know what I'm thinking until I start writing."

Sticky Essays in Action: Two Duke Applicants

Here's another example to help you understand what makes an essay sticky: Two students applied to Duke University—let's call them James and Ariya. Both submitted strong essays, but only one of them was admitted. I'll show you both essays, and you can try to determine which one got in.

James's Essay: The Sailing Challenge

When I was fourteen, I made a decision that changed my life. I, who had never been away from my family before, decided to spend my summer six thousand miles away at a Naval Academy in Michigan. I chose discipline, difficulty, and the outdoors over the comfort of home studying robotics and coding. Why? Because I wanted to test the waters: I wanted to learn to sail.

Before my parents dropped me off, they wiped every inch of my dorm room clean, thinking that would help. As they tearfully drove off, I was already wearing a stiff new military uniform and learning to march everywhere and how to ask permission to sit or eat. I was anonymous among cadets from Mexico, Brazil, and Russia—that is, until I took the tiller.

Two days after I arrived, I learned to sail. I was made skipper and in command of where the boat would go by using the tiller, which I had just learned was like the steering wheel of a car. I was happy with leading the crew; however, a minute after we set sail, I completely forgot about the tiller, sitting enthralled, listening to our sailing counselor talk. When she noticed that I had let the tiller spin randomly, she yelled, "James! You let go of the tiller!" I panicked, tried to grab the tiller, but it was too late, and our boat slowly capsized. In the water, everyone was yelling and thrashing while the counselor sat on top of the boat, shouting directions for us to bring the boat back upright. Back on shore, I desperately tried not to make eye contact with my drenched crew members who all knew my name now. "James! You let go of the tiller."

A few weeks later on a stormy day, the flags flapping wildly in the wind, our counselor told us that we were still going out. I was terrified as I got into the boat. At full sail, the boat was rocking violently from side to side as I sat frozen in my precious little seat just inches above raging waters.

I was in charge of the mainsail, so I pulled on the rope with all my might to make sure the sail was firm and steady. Tacking in strong winds meant having to stand up and quickly switch to the other side of the boat while the skipper turned the tiller abruptly to allow the boat to turn. As the boat turned, the sail would catch the full wind again and immediately jerk the boat to one side. Since I was in charge of the mainsail at all times, I had to pull on the rope hard so that the wind wouldn't blow the sail off, and lean all the way back to put weight on the side of the boat that was tilting upwards. During one tacking moment, the boat was at a 60-degree angle as I leaned all the way out with my entire backside exposed to the turbulent water below. Each wave that the boat rammed into was like driving into a speed bump at fifty miles an hour as torrents of water cascaded over us. Somehow I survived this frightening experience without capsizing the boat. By the end of that long, wet, arduous summer, whenever there was a stormy day, I volunteered to sail.

My experience at the Academy has stayed with me throughout high school, during the fourteen difficult AP courses I took, my biological research at UCSF and ASDRP where I failed more than I succeeded, and during the pandemic where, like so many students, I had to get over my feeling of isolation and force myself to reach out and support others.

Here's what I know now: If I never let go of the tiller, I can handle myself in any storm.

Priya's Essay: The Debate Deck Initiative

During my high school career, I successfully developed and implemented a comprehensive mobile application called "Debate Deck" which revolutionized speech and debate practice methodologies across multiple educational institutions. This technological solution addressed systemic inefficiencies in competitive debate training and ultimately enhanced performance outcomes for numerous students throughout our regional league.

The genesis of this project emerged from my observation that novice debaters at our school experienced significant difficulties maintaining structured practice routines without direct coach supervision. After conducting extensive research into existing debate training methodologies, I determined that the integration of mobile technology could provide a scalable solution to this pedagogical challenge.

Utilizing my foundational programming knowledge acquired through a summer coding intensive, I embarked upon the development of a multifaceted application incorporating the following key features: timed practice modules calibrated for different debate formats including Parliamentary, Public Forum, and Lincoln-Douglas styles; algorithmic generation of randomized topics and opposition arguments designed to simulate competitive scenarios; integrated recording capabilities enabling users to capture practice speeches and facilitate peer collaboration; comprehensive feedback systems incorporating specific evaluation criteria aligned with standard debate judging rubrics; and advanced analytics tracking improvements in speaking velocity, verbal filler reduction, and argument structural coherence.

The implementation phase required extensive beta testing protocols, user interface optimization based on feedback from team members, and iterative refinement of the application's core functionalities. I collaborated with our debate coach to ensure pedagogical alignment and worked with the school's IT department to address technical deployment considerations.

Using the Debate Deck app, our team's qualification rate for state championships doubled compared to previous years, with many competitors attributing their improved performance to consistent practice facilitated by the application. Additionally, I was invited to present my findings at the National

Debate Coaches Conference, where I delivered a presentation on "Technology Integration in Competitive Speech Education."

This experience has reinforced my commitment to leveraging technology for educational improvement. I believe that innovative solutions can address long-standing challenges in academic environments, and I look forward to continuing this type of impactful work in college and beyond.

Which Essay Was More Effective?

The two essays described different experiences—extracurricular initiative versus challenge in a summer program—but they both needed to be irresistibly sticky.

James got into Duke. Why? Because his essay had contrast and a payoff that evoked emotion, and his story was inspiring—"If I never let go of the tiller, I can handle myself in any storm." He expressed challenge, excitement, and confidence!

While Priya, even though she had a remarkable achievement, completely kills her story by

— revealing everything upfront (no suspense);

— using overly technical, pompous language;

— including too much boring detail about features;

— showing zero personality or emotion;

— ending with a generic, uninspiring conclusion; and

— making it sound like a research report instead of a personal story.

James, on the other hand, got into Duke because he wrote a compelling story about a turning point he had in the ninth grade! Even though she did something amazing, Priya wrote herself out of getting into Duke because her essay was technical and boring, while James's story fairly ripples with his determination and passion.

Digging for Diamonds: Finding Your Story

Now let's help you find your own sticky story. The following exercise, "Digging for Diamonds," is the process that all my successful students have used to write great essays. Remember what Hemingway said: "I don't know what I'm thinking until I start writing." That's exactly what you're going to do—explore what's in your heart and life experience through focused writing exercises.

For each prompt below, there's a starter sentence to get you flowing. Set a timer for five minutes per prompt and just write continuously without judgment. Remember to engage your writer self, not your editor self (go into a "no-judgment zone"). Think of your free writing like a faucet: You turn your writing on and then off after five minutes.

1. **Self-leadership.** Tell a story about when you showed self-leadership, meaning that you directed yourself to achieve something that was really hard for you to do. It could be raising your grades; learning a new musical skill; or excelling in martial arts, badminton, or volleyball. What did it take to achieve your goal? And what did you learn?

   Starter: The place where I've shown the most self-leadership is…

2. **Group leadership.** Tell a story about when you led your team or group to the next level. In other words, things changed because *you* took the helm. How did you do it? How did you contribute? And what did you learn from it?

   Starter: The group experience where I've shown the most initiative is…

3. **Challenge or adversity.** Tell about a personal challenge or adversity in your life—a sibling who is difficult or sick; a grandparent; your parents being immigrants, the difficulties they went through, and how their story has affected you; expectations that stress you out; your heritage; or a talent/passion that is central to who you are.

   Starter: To understand where I have overcome a challenge in my life, I need to tell you about my…

4. **Community service.** Tell a story about when you learned something from doing community service. How did you connect with the people you helped or worked with? Did it teach you something new or challenge any preconceived ideas you might have had?

   Starter: The service where I connected with others and learned the most was when…

5. **Academic initiative.** Tell a story about when you showed that you were fierce about learning—in a summer program, a particular class or outside of class, an experiment, a video, an invention, a hobby, or your personal reading or study. What hurdles

did you overcome in order to learn? How did you get through them? Did you create something from the experience?

Starter: I have been fierce about learning when it comes to…

Moving Forward

After completing the five freewriting exercises, read through them and choose the one that resonates the most with you. Then spend another twenty minutes expanding on it. This is Secret #7 from page 122 in action—when you're in the mood, finish writing the damn thing as quickly as you can!

This approach has given you a strong head start on your college application story. Use this momentum. Take a break, have something to eat, and then get right back to writing your essay. If you follow this process, you'll likely complete a solid draft very soon.

Remember Secret #8: Don't kill your babies by showing premature essays to anyone. Your parents will ask, and you can tell them about your progress, but don't have anyone read your drafts yet. It's too early for feedback. You want to write and explore freely at this point. Keep working on your essay, developing it over the summer, and you'll be well ahead of other applicants who wait until the last minute.

In my experience, the most successful college applicants are those who take the time to find their authentic story and tell it in a way that sticks with readers. Whether you're writing about academic initiative, leadership, overcoming challenges, community service, or passionate learning, your goal is the same: to create an essay that resonates emotionally and makes admissions officers fight for you in the committee room.

By following these "secrets" and digging for diamonds in your own life, you'll craft an essay that won't just be impressive—it will be irresistible.

Your Editor Self

As discussed earlier regarding sticky essays, there are two parts to being a writer. There's the "writer self," who digs for diamonds and finds his or her story without judgment. And there's the "editor self," who makes the story irresistible. Now that you've unleashed your writer self and drafted your essay, it's time to activate your editor self to transform your story into something truly sticky.

A Tale of Two Essays

To understand the power of effective editing, let's compare two essays on the same subject written by the same student, Karen. Essay A is the original unedited essay, and Essay B is the edited essay developed by using sticky strategies.

Essay A

I started attending the Red Cross Club meetings when I was a freshman. At that time, there were about five students in the club. I have worked hard to help build it, and now we have about thirty kids who come to the meetings regularly. Together we put on bake sales and sell T-shirts for catastrophes like what happened with Hurricane Matthew. Because of my hard work and dedication, I was chosen to be Youth Board Member for Alameda District's Red Cross Board of Directors. Last summer I spent six weeks being an intern at the Red Cross's main office in San Francisco. I mainly called people and companies for donations. All in all, the Red Cross has been central to my life, and I plan to continue doing it in college. The world is full of catastrophes, and the Red Cross and I will always be there.

Essay B

"The Red Cross is dumb." "It has nothing to do with me." The students I was talking with were right. As the Youth Board Member for the district's Red Cross, my job was to help students understand how the Red Cross helps in the world's worst situations. But since no teenager really bothers about the Red Cross, except maybe me and my five friends, how could I get my high school to care?

Remember how the amount of teenage deaths by drunk driving were made concrete by drawing the white outlines of dead teenagers on the sidewalk? My Red Cross Club members and I adapted that. We got twenty students dressed in red with dripping bloody faces to lie down all over campus with signs that said "This. Is. You. Come to the auditorium at noon today to find out why."

The auditorium was filled with noisy, gossipy kids, but I stilled them quickly when I turned down the lights and showed them a brief video of the current situation of 19 million refugees that are currently fleeing Syria, Honduras, Nigeria, Myanmar; 450,000 Syrian refugees have died so far, 50,000 of them children…Every hour a refugee dies…

But I knew that wasn't enough. As Mother Teresa once said, "Numbers are meaningless to people. You need to experience one person to act."

So when the lights came up, I asked, "If you know anyone who is a refugee or immigrant, please stand." The entire auditorium stood up. Then I asked, "If you come from an immigrant family, please remain standing." No one sat down. Then I asked, "If you are a refugee or immigrant, please remain standing." One fourth of my high school remained standing.

Then I brought Vata, a Syrian immigrant, forward. Very thin, wrapped in a long blue dress, her head covered, Vata began quietly. "When I was a little girl, my country was a beautiful warm green and brown place. I could walk anywhere and the world was my neighbor. Then the armies came and everything turned to dust and we were forced out of our homes and sent to foreign places. Everywhere we went, we were locked out or turned away. For months we wandered from refugee camp to refugee camp. Finally we heard that this one country was accepting Syrians, so we joined a boat filled to overflowing and we crossed the sea. At the time I had my first child, Argoes, so tiny and hungry, I held him to my breast so he could cry into my warm skin.

"At the end of an exhausting trip, where many of us got terribly seasick or died, we finally reached the other side. Once again everywhere we landed it was 'NO! Do not enter! You do not belong!' Sometimes it was with rifles pointed at us, sometimes with anger, sometimes with people just turning and walking away. Finally, at the last possible harbor, I stood at the prow and held my baby up for all to see—'For Argoes! Let us land, for this little baby!' A stranger yelled to us, 'Here! You can dock here.' But when we did, he said, 'Only for a little. We are full.' 'We will make room!' a woman said, interrupting him. She was wearing a Red Cross."

And then Vata said, "That is how I escaped so much hatred in my own land, so much hatred in the new lands, to wind up with my baby in the arms of the Red Cross."

We now have thirty-two active members in our Red Cross Club and have raised over $1,300 for refugees. But more importantly, I know now it isn't about caring for the Red Cross; it's about making room for Argoes.

What Makes an Essay Sticky?

These are two essays on the same subject, right? But one makes us care deeply, while the other leaves us cold. The second one, written by Karen, along with her being a National Merit finalist, helped her win the $100,000 scholarship from the University of Southern California. The first essay was her initial version before we edited it, using the "Sticky Strategies" you're about to learn.

You'll see exactly how we transformed Karen's essay, and these strategies will give you an edge when writing your own application essays. You're going to learn how to use X-ray vision on your own drafts to find easy ways to improve them.

Remember: **Sticky = understandable, memorable, and effective in changing readers' thoughts or behaviors.**

The Five Sticky Strategies

To edit your essay into something truly irresistible, focus on these five key strategies:

1. Find the knot.

2. Outsmart the villain.

3. Use hooks.

4. Use emotion to make people care.

5. Deliver a payoff.

Let's explore each of these in depth.

Find the Knot

This strategy is based on Aristotle's insight in *Poetics* that every well-written story begins with a knot (a problem) that is unraveled (solved) as the story progresses. So what is the knot in Karen's second essay?

> "As the Youth Board Member for the District's Red Cross, my job was to help students understand how the Red Cross helps in the world's worst situations.

But since no teenager really bothers about the Red Cross, except maybe me and my five friends, **how could I get my high school to care?"**

Karen's in charge of getting students involved in the Red Cross, but they all think it's boring and unimportant. She has to find a way to make it relevant to them. This is the problem she's attempting to solve in her essay.

Jade's Knot

To crystalize where I am coming from as a student and musician, I must share two secrets with you. First, I didn't get serious with violin until I was a sophomore and found out how much I had to learn.

At that time my fellow musicians were winning competitions and I was not; I had just been demoted from the first violin row in the Youth Symphony to the 20th chair. At that time I was invited to do a master class with world-famous violinist Haik Kaza-zyan; expecting him to give tips, I was devastated when he gave me reality: I had been playing violin for 7 years and still did not hold my bow correctly or make a consistently good sound. Reeling, I bravely confronted my beloved violin teacher a few days later, asking, "Why am I playing Brahms when I need proper technique?" Taken aback by my passion, he said, "I thought you were the best hobbyist I had." That is how I found David Chernyavsky, my current teacher, who taught me how to wage war.

For the second secret is this: I didn't learn how to become a truly good violinist until I learned to fight.

In my sophomore Honors Algebra class, my teacher said to us, "Don't just read math, fight it!" I have come to see, in my journey to Calculus, that each problem stands as its own monster, inspiring fear in untrained hearts. This is why we train—through class lectures to learn our weapons, in problem sets to practice, in tests to see if we can triumph.

This is what I learned from David: to conquer a musical piece, "don't just read music, wage war!"

To get in shape for a new piece, I first listen to the recordings of professionals playing it: they are already singing out their victory march, the final product of hours upon hours of battle. They have conquered the piece and made it theirs. Emboldened by their victory, I start low, like a scout spying out territory: I set the metronome at quarter speed and play through the piece, as my teacher taught me, "stupidly slowly." I need to nail the notes from the start. As I do my reconnaissance, I identify the particularly rebellious passages, setting them aside for special attention later. Then with the aid of my teacher, I figure out my first battle strategy: the fingerings. How exactly will I translate this mess of black ink on white paper to beautiful spasms of music and bone on metal strings? Slowly and patiently, I answer this question, sometimes taking days, even weeks to get through the entire piece. If I don't do this step correctly, I can sabotage my entire campaign. Napoleon once said that a war is won or lost in its preparation; I know this to be true with a piece of music. Skirmishes are done by dueling "technique specific" etudes or using "divide and conquer" to attack chords, or sometimes just drilling finger movements over and over again. My tuner is my sergeant, pointing out my mistakes in battle, always my honest companion. Only after all this do I start the daily practice, slowly chipping away at the fortress of the music, to take over, to make it my own, to conquer it.

This is how I ended up last summer as first violinist of the symphony at Tanglewood rehearsing "Rite of Spring" with the legendary conductor Paul Haas. Just for fun, Maestro Haas decided we should play one of the most complex sections without a conductor. As we played it, I could hear the orchestra breathing together, listening to each other, united in complete concentration. When we got through the section, played perfectly and in sync, I rested my violin, smiling. Tired and battle-scarred, yet triumphant, in that moment I fully understood how every great performance is the fruit of war.

In Jade's essay, her knot was actually her two "secrets." As she explained, "First, I didn't get serious with violin until I was a sophomore and found out how much I had to learn. The second secret is this: I didn't learn how to become a truly good violinist until I learned to fight." As soon as she sets up her problems, Jade immediately begins to unravel her knot when she tells us what she learned that helped her to solve it.

Now here's how to identify the knot in your own draft:

— Look for the main problem around which your story revolves.

— Make sure this problem is clearly articulated early in your essay.

— Then make sure the rest of your essay shows how you worked to solve this problem.

— If you don't have a clear problem yet, create one! A problem creates tension that keeps readers engaged.

Think of finding your knot like following a recipe. All you have to do is step one, then step two, etc. Or, it's like you're testing by throwing darts. Not all will stick, but some will. The ones that stick are the ones you'll use.

Outsmart the Villain

The "villain" we're always dealing with in college application essays is the "curse of knowledge." Admissions officers read hundreds to thousands of essays, and they often think they already know your story. In truth, they are unwittingly stereotyping you. This happens not just regarding ethnicity but also when it comes to activities like DECA, water polo, martial arts, speech and debate, and so on. They've heard it all before.

Stereotyping occurs because human beings are guessing machines. They assume they know something when they really don't. Do something unexpected, and it will break their stereotyping. What do you do when you don't have an extraordinary adversity or challenge such as death, addiction, or a disability? You apply this strategy and outsmart the villain.

How does Karen take on the villain in her essay? She confronts the stereotype head-on in a surprising way. She writes, "'The Red Cross is dumb.' 'It has nothing to do with me.' The students I was talking with were right." This direct acknowledgment of the negative perception of the Red Cross is startling and immediately sets her essay apart. The rest of her essay then proves that the Red Cross is actually interesting and important for high school students.

Similarly, Jade's violin essay breaks stereotypes from the beginning: "I didn't get serious with violin until I was a sophomore and found out how much I had to learn." This undercuts expectations about a young violinist. Her approach to improvement is unexpected too: "I didn't learn how to become a truly good violinist until I learned to fight." And then she explains how she learned that from her Algebra 2 class, which is also a surprising twist.

How do you outsmart the villain in your own essay? Your job is to deliberately break a pattern. You're trying to disrupt people's guessing machines. Here are some effective approaches:

— Make what you thought or did sound surprising.

Example: "All my friends hated the pandemic, but honestly I loved it."

— Use contrast, before and after.

Example 1: "Before I became an award-winning debater, I stuttered…"

Example 2: "I became a Boy Scout because my parents made me; I became an Eagle Scout because *it* made *me*."

— Do something unexpected.

Example: "All dressed up in a tuxedo, receiving a prestigious award at Carnegie Hall and sticking my tongue out at my mother. This journey is all her fault."

— Be so honest that it catches the reader off guard.

Example 1: "What people don't get about water polo is that it is, as my coach says, 'a lousy hard game to play.' The lower part of you is continually pumping a bicycle while the upper part is playing soccer and volleyball, and, unbelievably, it's done at the same time…"

Example 2: "I was the only Asian kid in my class who couldn't figure out for the life of me how to do Algebra 2…"

— Tell a vivid anecdote that makes the reader feel something.

Example 1: "I stood in front of my father trembling, hot tears running down my face. I had failed again."

Example 2: "One time during a particularly awful lesson with the maestro when everything I did was wrong, I excused myself, went into his private bathroom upstairs, knelt on the floor, and threw up awful bits of bile, exhaustion, and fear. I got up, washed my face, and, using a tissue to wipe away my angry tears, went back downstairs, stood on his hardwood floor, picked up my violin, cleared my throat, and began to practice again."

One easy way to begin your essay differently is to reverse how you originally thought to approach it. Instead of "Robotics is my life," try "Robotics is my death. Let me tell you why…"

To sum up, outsmart the villain of stereotyping by beginning your essays with the following:

— The unexpected

— A contrast that gets attention

— A surprise, like Jack meeting his father and not recognizing him (page 117)

— A mystery: How in the world did I get from there to here?

— A vivid anecdote that makes the reader feel how bad or good it really was

CHAPTER 17

Making Your Story Unforgettable

Now that you've learned how to find your knot and outsmart the villain, let's explore the remaining three strategies that will transform your essay from good to unforgettable.

Use Hooks

Using "hooks" to make your story real and believable is one of the best ways to make your essay come alive. Hooks are anything that helps your reader remember your story—concrete details, sensory descriptions, or contrasts that pop out to the reader. Think of this as the "Velcro Theory of Memory"—the more hooks in your story, the better it sticks!

The best hook is to *show* your story by using the five senses in your descriptions—taste, touch, smell, sight, and hearing. Help readers *feel* what it's like by avoiding the "curse of knowledge"—don't assume they have any idea what goes on in your world or why it's important.

In Karen's essay on the Red Cross, her use of hooks is masterful:

— Students with bloody faces lying on campus

— The entire student body standing up if they're immigrants

— Introducing Vata, a Syrian immigrant, with her vivid story

Look at this section of her essay, with the sensory hooks in boldface:

"**Very thin, wrapped in a long blue dress, her head covered**, Vata began quietly. "When I was a little girl, **my country was a beautiful warm green and brown place**. I could walk anywhere and the world was my neighbor. Then the armies came and everything turned to dust and we were forced out of our homes and sent to foreign places. Everywhere we went, we were locked out or turned away. For months we wandered from refugee camp to refugee camp. Finally we heard that this one country was accepting Syrians, so we joined a boat filled to overflowing and we crossed the sea. At the time I had **my first child, Argoes, so tiny and hungry, I held him to my breast so he could cry into my warm skin**. At the end of an exhausting trip, where many of us got terribly seasick or died, we finally reached the other side."

Here are some ways to use hooks in your college essay:

— **Use all five senses to describe experiences.** If your essay is about becoming a water polo leader, take us to a water polo game—let us live through it with you. If you're writing about a tennis match or a DECA tournament, help us feel what it's like to be there.

— **Show convincing details so readers believe you.** Here's how Jackie makes her volunteer time with Chewy in Tijuana (page 65) feel authentic: "On the last day I wanted to buy Chewy something special. I scooped him up and put him on my shoulders. I remember walking to the store in the glowing sunlight, my body feeling so filthy from the week of work and sweat, the ragged skyline of Tijuana behind us, and the weight of the happy little boy on my shoulders." Notice how Jackie uses touch and sight—glowing sunlight, ragged skyline, the weight of the happy boy on her shoulders—to draw a vivid picture.

— **Use contrast to make your details pop.** "When we got to the store I dropped Chewy to the ground and whispered to him, '*Usted puede comprar lo que quieres* (You can buy anything you want).' His little golden face lit up as he excitedly rushed to the fridge and grabbed an orange Fanta. There seemed to be nothing else in the store but dusty shelves."

— **Start in the middle of the action.** Here's part of Cindy's badminton essay, as she drops us right into the intensity of competition: "I'm toast. We're on opposite ends of a badminton court. Victoria, a poised, toned Canadian, taps her foot impatiently, eager to serve her eighteenth point. Three points left to a clean win. When the umpire motions for play to begin, Victoria serves. I want the pressure on her, I attack right away.

The bird can't go up, so I play flat, I play fast. Three shots later, she falters, forcing a shot that goes wide. I'll take it."

In summary, use hooks effectively by employing these strategies:

- ✦ Engage all five senses.

- ✦ Create vivid contrasts.

- ✦ Include concrete details.

- ✦ Use telling anecdotes.

- ✦ Begin in the middle of the action.

Use Emotion to Make People Care

Using emotion isn't about manipulating people's feelings the way a tearjerker movie does. Instead, the goal of making your essay "emotional" is to make admissions officers care about you and your story. Consider the following two openings about a student's badminton experience.

Version A: "It turned out I was very successful as a badminton player—out of forty-nine matches, I won 87% of them and went on to become the Pan Am Singles Champion. I owe all of this to the grace of my talent and work ethic, but especially to my mentor Coach Lang, who taught me to 'never let the bird touch the ground.'"

Version B: "I'm toast. We're on opposite ends of a badminton court. Victoria, a poised, toned Canadian, taps her foot impatiently, eager to serve her eighteenth point. Three points left to a clean win. I think about my old Coach Lang back home, her words to me as a ten-year-old: 'It doesn't matter how good your opponent is, you're not going to give them an easy time. Annoy them to death if you have to. At the brink of losing, you're a dead man anyway.' I do feel like a dead man—stuffy nose, fever—my first Pan Am singles appearance and I'm a mess…Five months later, as Coach Lang begins her chemotherapy, I pass her an envelope. 'For Strength,' lettered on a handwritten note. 'Under 17 Girls' Singles Pan Am Champion,' engraved on the gold medal wrapped inside. I present her my highest honor. She taught me the greatest lesson: Magic happens when you do not let the bird hit the ground."

The difference is striking. In Version A, you're given statistics that engage your analytical mind. In version B, you're carried along with the story, opening your heart because you feel and care. One is cerebral, the other emotional.

Remember: You become eligible for a top college with your mind, but you get in with your heart.

Making people care: the Mother Teresa effect. Karen's essay brilliantly uses what I call the "Mother Teresa effect." Mother Teresa said, "If I look at the one, I will act." Charitable groups know that donors respond better to individuals than to abstract causes. That's why you always see one hungry child, one sad dog, or one cancer patient in fundraising appeals—not statistics about world hunger or disease. "If I feel the one, I will act."

Remember the "curse of knowledge" that makes readers think they know all about your club, activity, or contribution when they really don't? Introducing one person who embodies your idea, club, or contribution in a moving way can break through this barrier. Consider the students mentioned in this book who made their essays emotional:

— Karen introduced Vata and her baby, Argoes, representing Syrian refugees.

— Jackie focused on her connection with one Mexican boy, Chewy.

— Andrew's essay about Boy Scouts zeroed in on "the youngest kid in the room."

— Jack unflinchingly talked about his dad's AIDS and death.

Andrew's The Youngest Kid in the Room essay makes us care by focusing on a specific moment and person:

When I was first a Tenderfoot, I went away to Boy Scouts camp for the first time. I hadn't much liked Cub Scouts, and I was trying out Boy Scouts to see if it was any better. But I hated being away from home, and the older boys seemed to be having all the fun. We had dodgeball teams, but the younger Scouts didn't get to play much. However, I loved dodgeball and was a good player at my school, so I kept begging the older scouts to let me play. No one would let me join. I kept on asking until something happened that made all the difference. An older Scout reached out to me and said, 'Here, take my spot.' I was so ecstatic, I stumbled all over myself getting into the game, for I couldn't believe that I was given the opportunity to play dodgeball with the older Scouts.

This connection to one individual creates an emotional resonance that statistics and general descriptions simply cannot match.

Making your essay emotional. Instead of writing about an overall "club experience" where you solved a problem and learned something, zoom in on one person who shows how you made a difference. If you're writing about transforming the computer club, for instance, focus on one member whose experience demonstrates the impact you've had.

Deliver a Payoff

The final and perhaps most important strategy is to tell a story that shows a payoff. Unravel the knot, solve the problem, and leave us with a real insight. Stories with a payoff make us care and inspire us to act. This is the whole point of your college essay; when admissions officers care, they act by admitting you to their college.

All good stories are a series of problems that you solved to get somewhere. But the getting there—the payoff—is what's crucial. Here are some examples of powerful payoffs:

Karen's payoff: "We now have thirty-two active members in our Red Cross Club and have raised over $11,000 for refugees. But more importantly, I know now it isn't about caring for the Red Cross; it's about making room for Argoes." Not only did she get students to care about the Red Cross, but she herself gained a new understanding of why it matters. This evolution in her thinking provides a fresh and insightful conclusion.

Jackie's payoff: "But when I returned home, I had changed. I volunteered much more, worked to change the environment, and started my own company to give back. Chewy is forever running alongside my bus, calling 'Yackie! Yackie!' I carry him always on my shoulders. I say to him, 'I will not take the easy way. I will speak up.'" Her experience taught her to stand up for what she believes despite peer pressure.

Andrew's payoff: "I can only hope he passes it on and that he learned like I did, to always reach out to the youngest kid in the room." Andrew learned the essence of being a Boy Scout—to always reach out to those who need inclusion.

Terry's payoff: "After the tournament, I found out that of the sixty-four debaters chosen to advance, I was sixty-five. It was my coach who told me, and she added, 'Thanks for helping out; I know it wasn't easy.' I looked at her and grinned, 'I guess I learned how to be the bigger number today.'" Terry learned something even more valuable than advancing in the tournament—he learned how to support others and find meaning in defeat.

A Complete Example: Dixon's Violin Essay

Let's look at how all these strategies come together in this successful essay that helped Dixon get into Cornell:

When I was four years old, my mother gave me a tiny violin, which she felt was a gift. For the next six years, my childhood was spent with my mother yelling at me to practice violin every day. Daily practice sessions were preceded by foreboding dread, incessant screaming, and tears. Each day, my mother patiently sat by my side as I practiced. In response, my cunning six-year-old self took "bathroom breaks" every ten minutes to avoid the violin. During my weekly private lessons, my mother took notes in her bright green notebook, frantically jotting down Mr. Qi's every word.

One time when I was in third grade, during a particularly difficult lesson, I repeatedly struggled with a challenging sixteenth-note passage. Frustrated and angry, I excused myself and retreated to my teacher's half bathroom. I screamed into a towel, and wiping the tears out of my eyes, I calmly returned to the studio to continue my lesson.

Then, when I was ten years old, my mother enrolled me in my first orchestra, the Elementary Advanced Orchestra held at my local middle school. At the first rehearsal, I sat in my seat, churlishly waiting amid fifty other musicians for our practice to begin. Mr. Conway, who turned out to be a kind and inspiring teacher, strode into the room and motioned for the violinist next to me to play the tuning "A" note. Until that moment, I had never played with other instruments, for I had always practiced by myself or with my private teacher. And when that violinist played that single note, fifty other instruments joined in unison, the harmonies swelled up into the ceiling of the auditorium. It felt as if that one note had expanded my heart. After that, violin practice became somehow easier.

A few years later, when I was thirteen and wandering aimlessly around a convention hall by myself, I came upon a violin vendor. My school orchestra was performing in the National Orchestra Festival, and we were waiting to play "Vanishing Pointe" by Richard Meyer. At the vendor's sales booth, I had never seen so many beautiful violins in one place. Since the vendor had no customers, he said to "go ahead and try one." I was curious to hear how the new, shiny German violins would sound compared to my vintage Italian one. So, I picked one up, tuned it, and began to play the opening of the piece the orchestra was performing that afternoon. As I played, one of my fellow violinists heard me, came over, and joined me playing one of the vendor's violins.

Gradually, one by one, every member of the violin section came over, picked up a violin, and joined me in an ad hoc concert. Some of them were my closest friends, while others I had never spoken to. Some were eager, while others were reluctant. But eventually, all of them joined in playing our set for the afternoon.

When we had finished, the convention hall filled with applause. We had been so lost in the music that we didn't realize everyone had stopped talking, instead listening to our performance. Surprised by the applause, we burst into laughter.

Years later, as I am standing onstage to receive the American Protégé award, I remember that petulant four-year-old boy sweatily holding a tiny violin, not wanting to play. I smile at my mother in the audience. And as I smile, my heart swells as if from one note perfectly played. Then I hear them, my forty fellow violinists playing "Vanishing Pointe" for me, all of us laughing together out of sheer joy. *This is the music I will bring to college.*

Dixon's essay succeeds because it

— establishes a clear knot (the struggle with violin practice);

— breaks the stereotype by contrast (not the typical "I hated music from the start" essay);

— uses vivid hooks (screaming into towels, endless bathroom breaks, the magic of the spontaneous convention hall concert);

— makes us (the reader) care about the struggling young violinist and his journey; and

— delivers a beautiful payoff (the transformation from reluctance to joy and connection).

The Sticky Strategies Checklist

The most successful college essays are those that move beyond mere accomplishments to reveal authentic growth, connection, and insight. By applying the following five strategies, you can transform your initial draft into a compelling essay that admissions officers won't forget.

Learning to tell stories that stick is a skill that will serve you well beyond the college application process. The ability to make others care, to communicate memorably, and to inspire action will be valuable throughout your academic career and professional life. All great leaders, innovators, and changemakers know how to tell stories that inspire others to join in their mission.

Your college essay is the centerpiece of your application. Make it stick by using the following checklist to identify areas for improvement after you've completed your first draft.

- ✓ **Strategy #1: Did I untie the knot?** To find the knot, first find your problem. You may not feel that you have one yet, but look for a problem related to your chosen subject—like Karen's "How do I get high school students to care about the Red Cross?"

- ✓ **Strategy #2: Did I outsmart the villain?** To outsmart the villain of stereotyping, begin your essays with one of these:

  — The unexpected ("My friends hated the pandemic. I loved it.")

  — A contrast that gets attention ("Before I became a tap dancer, I limped.")

  — A surprise (like Jack meeting his father and not recognizing him)

  — A mystery ("How in the world did I get from there to here?")

  — A vivid anecdote that makes the reader feel how bad or good something really was (like Dixon yelling into a towel because he hated piano practice)

- ✓ **Strategy #3: Did I use sticky hooks?** Use every hook you can to make others feel how it feels to *you*. The following hooks will bring out concrete details in your story:

— Using all five senses to describe an experience

— Using contrast, before and after, so the reader can vividly see something change

— Using compelling anecdotes

— Giving concrete details

— Starting in the middle of the action as the knot begins to unravel

✓ **Strategy #4: Did I use emotion to make people care?** Using emotion isn't about pushing people's emotional buttons, like some kind of movie tearjerker. Rather, the goal of making messages "emotional" is to make people connect with you and care.

✓ **Strategy #5: Did I deliver a payoff?** Tell a story with a payoff. Unravel the knot, solve the problem, and leave us with a real insight—like Mai's "You ain't seen nothing yet," showing confidence and future promise.

PART III

Proving Your Superstar Status

CHAPTER 18

The Wheel— When Everything Connects

"When the center holds, everything connects, and though storms may rage on the periphery at the heart is wisdom."

—RICHARD STROZZI HECKLER

I sadly watched a YouTube video called "Why I Got Rejected from Stanford." Here was this amazing Asian American girl, Izzy, detailing all that she'd done—4.11 GPA, 1580 on her SATs, 11 APs with 5-point test scores, countless awards and trophies for Olympiads and quiz bowls, president of this, director of that. She truly was a Busy Bee, a Pied Piper, and a Cheerleader all rolled into one—but it still wasn't enough. She didn't get into her dream school, Stanford.

She blamed her essay, saying that she'd written on the wrong subject and also hadn't faced enough adversity. But I saw something else. Her résumé—filled to the brim with stellar activities, great awards, and leadership—was so stuffed that I was overwhelmed. Her recommenders, while all agreeing she was a superstar, couldn't quite capture who she was. I couldn't figure out what mattered to Izzy. Consequently, I got absolutely no feeling for her at all. Nothing but too much info. But as I read through her résumé, I saw one important detail that I would have pulled out and put in the center, turning her résumé inside out.

Izzy had quietly started a weekly generative AI program for disabled kids to get them excited about machine learning. It was very successful, and the model she'd started was being used by three other middle schools as well as the school district itself. I would have put this remarkable project at the center of her story, and then all her multiple achievements would flow from it—not necessarily directly from her AI project, but from what it clearly said about *her*. Here was a girl who was already a brilliant young educator; the quiz bowls she won, the tutoring clubs she set up, the science fairs she won were all deeply connected to her generous and far-seeing heart. She understood very clearly that if disabled people could own AI and machine learning, they would transform their world.

Alas, I wasn't Izzy's college application coach, and this YouTube video was from two years prior. But I *could* transform my own students' paths by making sure they knew what was most important to them and how everything fit together.

Elizabeth sat across from me, surrounded by pieces of her application—her remarkable project of teaching art to special needs students, her essay about transforming her school's art club, her national art awards. "I have all these pieces," she said, "and I think I am ready to show my teachers for recommendations, but something's missing. They don't feel…connected."

I smiled and drew a wheel on the paper between us. "That's because we haven't put your story at the center yet. Once we do that, everything else will align naturally."

The Power of the Center

Think of your college application as a wheel. Most students scatter their achievements around the rim, hoping the sheer number of accomplishments will impress. But a wheel's strength comes from its center—the hub that connects everything.

Your story is that center.

Personal Story Wheel Diagram

Finding Your Center

For Elizabeth, her center wasn't just "art"—it was *using* art to create belonging. Once she realized this, she saw that

— her art club leadership showed vision;

— her special needs program demonstrated impact;

— her summer program choices made sense for her major;

— her essays resonated with purpose; and

— even her choice of a major (art therapy) aligned perfectly.

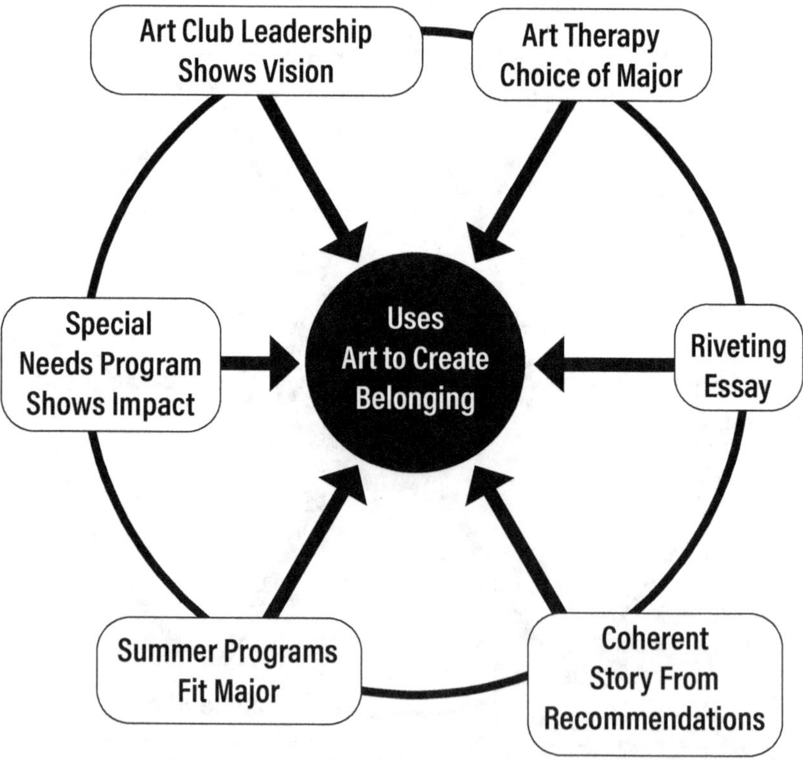

Elizabeth did the wheel process because she wanted to present a coherent story to her recommenders and on her application.

The Natural Alignment

When you put your authentic story at the center, here's what can happen:

— Activities become more than a list; they show your values in action.

— Leadership roles demonstrate your way of making change.

— Service reflects your unique contribution.

— Academic choices support your path.

— Summer programs deepen your impact.

— Awards validate your journey.

— Essays write themselves (well, almost!).

— Interviews feel natural.

Let's take a look at how a couple of different students found their own centers. Akira created a Coding Club.

Akira's center: Using technology to build community

— Coding club → Created belonging through shared creation

— App development → Solved real school problems by creating an app for AP teachers for assignments and prep for the AP test

— Leadership style → Built teams and celebrated success

— Summer program → Deepened technical skills

— Essay → Showed personal growth through leading

— Recommendations → Highlighted both Akira's technical and human skills

Charlotte was an injured track star who, instead of feeling sorry for herself, became cheerleader and strategist for her team.

Charlotte's center: Transforming setbacks into opportunities

— Team role → From player to strategic leader

— Service → Created athlete mentoring program

— Leadership → Built support systems for others

— Essay → Journey from personal loss to community gain

— Recommendations → Showed resilience and innovation

Personal Story Wheel Worksheet

Fill in each section to connect your experiences to your center story.

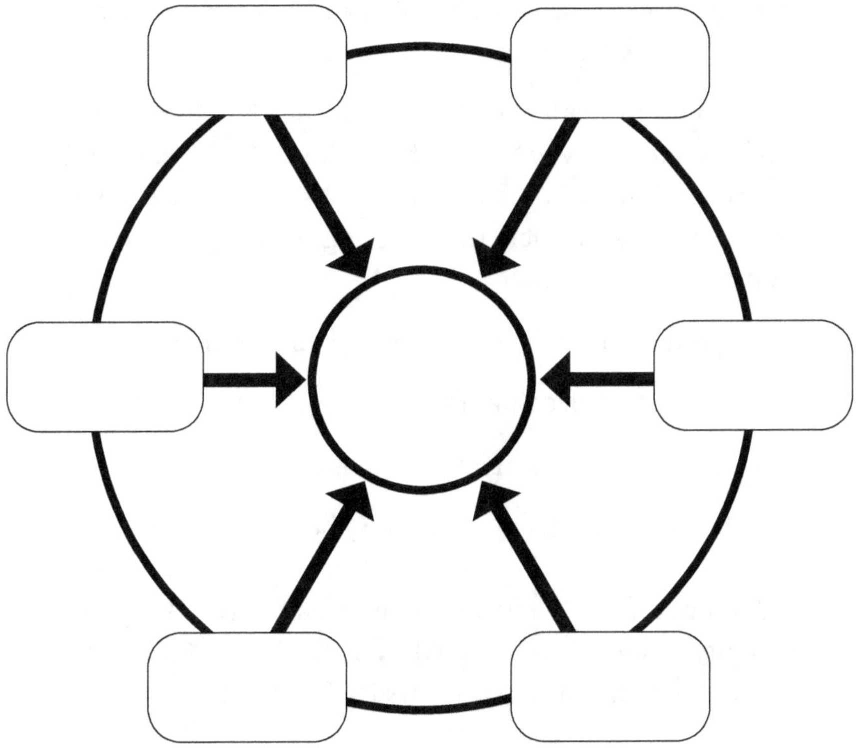

Finding Your Own Center Story

Ask yourself these four questions:

1. Is there a reoccurring story emerging in everything that I do?

2. What gets me so involved that it makes me lose track of time?

3. How do I naturally help others?

4. What problems do I love solving?

Once you've found your center story, everything should connect back to it naturally. If something feels forced or disconnected, it probably is.

Why does this matter? Colleges aren't just looking at what you've done—they're looking for a sense of coherence and character. Elite colleges want to see a student who knows who they are and where they're going. When your application has a strong center

— admissions officers understand you quickly;

— your story becomes memorable;

— your potential impact becomes clear; and

— your fit with their community becomes obvious.

Put your authentic story at the center, and everything else will align naturally. Just as Meister Eckhart said, get the center right and the circle draws itself perfectly.

CHAPTER 19

Evidence Wins the Day

A few years ago, I was asked to judge a scholarship competition for a Chinese organization. I was flattered that they asked me, and I read all 147 applications carefully. The students seemed very good. Their extracurriculars ranged from starting a mental health therapy group in their high school to creating a volleyball team to organizing a huge fundraiser.

But there was one ninth-grade boy, Lawrence, who stood out from all the tenth and eleventh graders who'd submitted applications. He went around his neighborhood getting broken and unusable eyeglasses from everyone, which he then fixed with his grandpa's help and gave to the homeless. With his essay, Lawrence attached a photograph of a big cardboard box filled to overflowing with broken eyeglasses. The other thing he did was teach a disabled little girl how to play the piano, and he'd attached a short video of himself teaching her, showing the joy on her parents' faces as she played for them.

When I read his essay, looked at the video, and saw the photograph, I was genuinely moved by this fourteen-year-old taking the initiative to go to every house in his neighborhood collecting hundreds of broken glasses. Even though the other 146 students had done a lot of wonderful things, not one person thought to enclose any evidence of what they'd actually done. Yes, there were recommendations, but not one of them mentioned what a student said they'd done in their résumé or story—not a recommendation letter or a photograph or even an award backing it up. The only thing they had was their own "story" about it.

I gave the scholarship to Lawrence because I believed him, and I was moved by what he had done. That experience taught me a great deal. You can say whatever you want in the story you tell, but you need to have evidence that your story is true. Evidence wins the day.

What gives things resonance and depth is when you back up what you did so that the reader believes you.

This need for evidence connects directly to our "wheel concept." When your story forms a strong center, your evidence becomes the spokes that support it. Without those spokes, even the most compelling center cannot hold weight in the admissions process. This section is about exactly that: getting evidence so the reader will believe you—that is, getting sticky recommendations, doing sticky interviews, and creating a remarkable résumé that quickly showcases and backs up what you've done.

However, I need to point out that the current reality is that you can't really send in photographs unless colleges request them. You also can't send a video unless they request it. Fortunately, colleges are increasingly requesting two-minute videos instead of interviews, allowing you to visually showcase your remarkable project. When Linda did her two-minute video for Pomona on how she'd transformed a moribund Speech & Debate Club into the largest and most successful club on campus (page 62) throughout her four years in high school, she could show four years of yearbook pictures to back it up. We could actually see the transformation from five lonely students to fifty grinning kids, some of them holding trophies.

Colleges want to see specific evidence that validates your story: teacher recommendations that explicitly mention your projects and their impact, awards that confirm your achievements, and concrete details about the change you've created. Just as your essays need to be sticky to make admissions officers care, your evidence needs to be sticky as well—specific, memorable, and emotionally compelling.

The key thing that gives evidence is a recommendation. It's important that your teacher or mentor knows enough about you to back up that you did something remarkable and made a difference. And if you do something successful outside of school, like Jeff did with his after-school basketball program for underserved kids, it's essential that you have the adult in charge (principal, supervisor, etc.) write a rave review about your work.

In the following chapters, you will learn how to give your recommender the kind of information needed to write you a wonderful recommendation. I'll show you different recommendation versions, and you'll learn how to do a sticky résumé showcasing your remarkable story front and center. And lastly, you'll see how to prepare for and do an enjoyable and successful qualitative college interview.

It wasn't until I oversaw that scholarship competition that I realized how crucially emotion, story, evidence, and recommendations are intertwined—and how important emotion is in order for you to be accepted. It's not so different from those emotional Budweiser commercials with Clydesdale horses, their enormous hooves moving slowly through the crisp snow with gorgeous music that makes viewers tear up just to buy beer. Or those heartwarming Coca-Cola holiday ads where families of polar bears make you want to find joy in sharing a bottle of Coke with your family.

These commercials sell through feelings. Your essay does too—and recommendations back up those feelings.

As a recommender wrote about one of my students, "At first Alicia seemed like a plain covered book in my history class. But increasingly, as I read her essays and papers, as she contributed in class and as I spoke to her after class, I felt her nuanced intelligence and initiative. Getting to know her was like opening a boring book and discovering magic. Never, in all my years as a teacher, have I been more moved by what a student has done. I truly believe you will find her not just a top student but one of the best you've ever had. Let me run through quickly some of the changes she and her leadership team have brought to our high school and why they matter to us so much."

He goes on to give a string of evidence showing why she's a superstar. That was a sticky recommendation! And the first step in creating one for yourself is to create a story-driven résumé.

CHAPTER 20

Making Excellence Visible— The Story-Driven Résumé

Here's a truth that most students miss: Your résumé isn't just a list—it's a story. And like any compelling story, it needs a beginning (where you started), a middle (how you grew), and an end (your own remarkable achievement).

Your résumé is one of the most powerful tools for showing the coherence of your wheel. Rather than scattering achievements around the rim, your résumé should clearly demonstrate how everything connects to your center story.

Think about those critical first fifteen seconds when an admissions officer glances at your résumé. In that brief time span, three things must be instantly clear:

1. What makes you different

2. Proof of your excellence

3. A coherent story of your progression

Most superstar students produce résumés that look something like this:

ABHAY PATEL

Honors and Awards

— Distinction: AP Scholar Award (2018)

— National Merit Scholarship Program: Commended Student (2018)

— California Scholarship Federation (2017, 2018, 2019)

— DECA District Competition: 1st Place Business Management (2018)

— DECA State Competition: 3rd Place Entrepreneurship (2018)

— President's Volunteer Service Award: Gold Medal (2018)

Business Honors and Awards

— DECA International Competition: Finalist (2018)

— Future Business Leaders of America: Regional Winner (2018)

— Entrepreneurship Competition: County 2nd Place (2018)

— Junior Achievement Company of the Year (2018)

Positions of Leadership

— DECA Training Coordinator: Lincoln High School (2017, 2018)

— President: Future Business Leaders of America (2018, 2019)

— Vice President: Entrepreneurship Club (2017, 2018)

— Captain: Academic Decathlon Team (2018, 2019)

Community Service

— Volunteer Tutor: Boys & Girls Club (2016–2018)

— Food Bank Volunteer (2017–2018)

— Senior Center Assistant (2016–2017)

Technology

— Developer: iOS App DECA Prep (2017, 2018)

Additional sections follow with school activities, academics, etc.

Notice something? Abhay's most remarkable achievement—creating an iOS app that transformed DECA training for more than seventy students and spread to three other schools—is buried at the bottom as a single line. If you blinked, you'd miss it entirely.

This is a classic "list without a story" résumé. It documents what Abhay did but fails to showcase who he became and the remarkable impact he made. Most importantly, it buries his superstar achievement.

From List to Story: The Transformation

Now imagine if Abhay's résumé looked like this instead:

ABHAY PATEL

— Evolution: From DECA Member
to Business Innovation Leader

— [iOS App "DECA Prep":
Used by 200+ students across four schools]

MY REMARKABLE PROJECT

Created comprehensive DECA training app that revolutionized competition preparation:

— Identified inefficiencies in traditional mentoring
system (70+ students, handful of mentors)

— Self-taught iOS development to solve real business
education challenges

— Designed scalable solution with video tutorials,
scheduling system, and progress tracking

— App adopted by three neighboring schools'
DECA programs

— First-year participants scored 28% higher in
competitions

— Link: [App Store URL & demo video]

MY PROGRESSION STORY

The Beginning (9th–10th Grade)

— Joined DECA as novice competitor

— Struggled with limited mentor access like other beginners

— Recognized systemic problem in competition preparation

Taking Leadership (10th–11th Grade)

— Advanced to DECA Training Coordinator role

— Managed training for 70+ younger members

— Earned 1st Place District, 3rd Place State in Business Management

— Qualified for DECA International Competition

Creating Bigger Impact (11th–12th Grade)

— Developed innovative technology solution for mentoring challenges

— Led team to state recognition for "innovative leadership"

— Expanded impact beyond school to district-wide adoption

— Transformed from competitor to business systems innovator

Additional sections follow with progression of school activities, academics, etc.

See the difference? This story-driven résumé

— immediately shows what makes Abhay unique (business leadership + technology innovation);

— places his remarkable project front and center;

— tells a coherent story of growth from member to innovator; and

— shows measurable impact and scalability.

This demonstrates exactly what admissions officers mean when they say they're looking for students who will make an impact. Abhay's revised résumé doesn't just document his accomplishments; it shows his evolution from participant to leader to business innovator.

Not All Recognition Is Equal

Another key element of your résumé is understanding the hierarchy of awards and recognitions. At top schools, some achievements carry more weight than others.

Superstar awards:

— First place in national/international competitions

— National Merit Finalist

— Top awards in prestigious competitions (International Science and Engineering Fair, DECA International, etc.)

— Field-specific recognition (AMC 12 Distinguished, National Chemistry Olympiad, etc.)

Strong but common awards:

— AP Scholar with Distinction

— National Honor Society

— President's Volunteer Service Award

— Honor Roll/California Scholarship Federation Award

Here's the brutal truth: That President's Volunteer Service Award that took you 100+ hours to earn? For elite colleges, it's become part of the "Asian stereotype" unless you have a remarkable story behind it. The same applies to AP Scholar awards and Honor Society memberships—they're *expected*, not distinguishing.

The Star-to-Superstar Résumé Template

To help you create a résumé that tells your personal progression story, here's a template that works for any remarkable project and that you submit in the "additional information" section of the common app and for interviews and scholarships.

FROM STAR TO SUPERSTAR: YOUR PROGRESSION RÉSUMÉ TEMPLATE

[YOUR NAME]

Your Journey: From [Starting Point] to [Remarkable Achievement]

[Link to Evidence: Website/Video/Article/etc.]

YOUR REMARKABLE PROJECT

Brief description of your innovative contribution:

— A problem you identified

— The solution you created

— Your impact on others

— Evidence of success

— Link to proof (if applicable)

YOUR PROGRESSION STORY

The Foundation (9th–10th grade)

— First involvement in your key activity

— Early recognition/achievements

— Initial leadership or responsibility

Building Skills (10th–11th grade)

— Key learning experiences

— Increasing responsibilities

— Notable accomplishments

Transformation (11th–12th grade)

— Taking leadership

+ Major role or position

+ What you changed or improved

+ Measurable impact

— Creating something remarkable

+ Your innovative project/solution

+ A problem you solved

+ Impact on others

+ Evidence of success

AWARDS SHOWING GROWTH

[Stack chronologically to show progression]

9th Grade

— Initial recognitions

10th Grade

— Growing achievements

11th Grade

— Major accomplishments

12th Grade

— Highest achievements

— Recognition of your remarkable project

LEADERSHIP EVOLUTION

9th grade: [Beginning role]

10th grade: [Growing responsibility]

11th grade: [Major leadership]

12th grade: [Innovative contribution]

KEY ACTIVITIES

— Main activity and progression of involvement

— Supporting activities, showing dedication

— Hours/weeks of involvement for each year

EVIDENCE OF IMPACT

[Concrete numbers/results]

— Growth statistics for remarkable project

— People affected

— Money raised

— Problems solved

— Recognition received

ACADEMIC EXCELLENCE

[Standard but important info]

— GPA (weighted/unweighted)

— SAT/ACT scores

— Key academic awards

Now let's see how this template works for different types of projects.

The Innovation Story: Abhay's iOS App

Abhay created technology to solve a real problem in DECA. His progression shows how he

— started as a helpful DECA member;

— grew into leadership positions;

— identified a key challenge;

— created a technological solution; and

— expanded its impact beyond his school.

The Research Journey: Terry's Story

TERRY

From science student to published HIV/AIDS researcher

[Link to Journal of Emerging Investigators Publications]

REMARKABLE PROJECT

Developed novel approach to HIV/AIDS treatment:

— Designed new methodology for treatment

— Created virtual screening techniques

— Publication pending in Journal of Emerging Investigators

— Gave a presentation at the American Chemical Society Conference

PROGRESSION STORY

— Started as a science fair competitor with early interest in chemistry

— Grew to be part of a research team at a prestigious program

— Created novel HIV/AIDS treatment approach, with pending publication

— Impact: research contributing to medical understanding

The Community Builder: Dae's Impact

DAE

From science enthusiast to scientific community builder

REMARKABLE PROJECT

Created a unified scientific competition ecosystem from middle school through high school

— Transformed separate science teams into a cohesive community

— Led his school's Science Bowl team to second place nationally

— Restarted a middle school science program

— Built sustainable leadership structure across multiple teams

— Raised $5,000 for competition programs (travel to Bowls, Olympiads, etc.)

PROGRESSION STORY

— Started as individual competitor in science competitions

— Grew to team captain and coach

— Created a comprehensive academic competition system

— Reached out to middle school in creating competition preparation system

— Impact: multiple teams achieving national recognition

Making Your Remarkable Project Visible

No matter what type of remarkable project you've created, here are five key strategies for making it stand out in your college application.

1. **Put it at the top.** Don't bury your achievement in a list of activities. Give it prime positioning.

2. **Show progression.** Make your growth journey visible, from your initial involvement to your remarkable achievement.

3. **Include specific numbers.** The people affected, the money raised, the growth achieved, and the awards won—these specifics make your impact real.

4. **Link to evidence.** Whenever possible, include links to proof: publications, videos, websites, news coverage.

5. **Use bold statements.** Don't be shy about your achievement! Frame it clearly—"created," "founded," "transformed."

The Evidence Test

Remember that scholarship competition that I judged where Lawrence, the ninth grader, won because he'd included a photo of his eyeglasses collection project? Your résumé should pass the same test. Ask yourself these questions:

— Would someone believe this achievement is real based on my résumé?

— Have I included specific details that prove my impact?

— Does my progression story make logical sense?

— Is there clear evidence backing my claims about what I've done?

— Can I link to or provide tangible proof?

Your résumé isn't just for documenting what you've done; it's to prove the person you've become. When your résumé tells a coherent story of growth that culminates in a remarkable achievement, it becomes powerful evidence that you're not just a star student but a genuine superstar who will make an impact in college and beyond.

Remember: In those critical first fifteen minutes, admissions officers should immediately see what makes you different, proof of your excellence, and your coherent story of growth. Make those minutes count by showcasing your remarkable project and the journey that led to it.

Here are more examples of star-to-superstar résumés, showing the same achievements used in different ways. The key difference in these cases isn't fabricating achievements but thoughtfully organizing authentic experiences around a meaningful center that represents one's true passions and contribution.

Example 1: STEM student with music background

Achievement list:

— Orchestra member for four years

— Science fair winner

— Computer Science Club president

— Created an iOS app

— Summer internship at research lab

— Volunteer tutor

"Innovation Through Intersection" résumé:

REMARKABLE PROJECT:

Creating a music practice app that transformed rehearsal methods

— Identified inefficiencies in traditional practice techniques

— Combined technical skills and musical knowledge

— Developed a solution used by multiple school orchestras

— Demonstrated innovation at the intersection of arts and technology

"Scientific Leadership" résumé:

REMARKABLE PROJECT:

Building an inclusive STEM community

— Revitalized school's Computer Science Club from five to thirty members

— Organized a peer tutoring science program for underclassmen

— Created resources to make coding accessible for beginners

— Applied technical skills to develop educational tools

— Orchestra experience contributed to collaborative mindset

Example 2: Community builder with athletics background

Achievement list:

— Varsity basketball team captain

— Student government representative

— School food drive founder

— Hospital volunteer (300+ hours)

— Summer leadership program as participant

— Academic honor roll

"Health Advocacy" résumé:

REMARKABLE PROJECT:

Transforming youth health access

— Used the school's athletics platform to create an awareness campaign

— Organized health screenings at school tournaments

— Connected hospital experience with community outreach

— Initiated a food drive focused on nutritional equity

— Led leadership program for developing health advocacy skills

"Inclusive Leadership" résumé:

REMARKABLE PROJECT:

Creating belongingness in school community

— Transformed basketball team culture from competitive to collaborative

— Initiated "bench player recognition" program

— Used student government position to give voice to underrepresented groups

— Founded a food drive to address economic disparities

— Hospital volunteering contributed to developing empathy skills

Example 3: Service-oriented student with academic focus

Achievement list:

— National Honor Society member

— ESL tutor for immigrant families

— Took part in research project on local water quality

— Started a recycling program

— Took part in summer environmental program

— Had poetry published in school magazine

"Environmental Justice" résumé:

REMARKABLE PROJECT:

Creating community environmental awareness

— Water quality research focused on underserved neighborhoods

- Recycling program designed to engage multicultural community

- ESL tutoring including environmental vocabulary component

- Poetry used as medium for environmental advocacy

- Academic achievements used as foundation for research

"Cross-Cultural Communication" résumé:

REMARKABLE PROJECT:

Building bridges between cultures

- ESL tutoring was transformed into mutual cultural exchange

- Created multilingual environmental education materials

- Explored themes of cultural identity through poetry

- Research project included multilingual community surveys

- Recycling program used as practical application of cross-cultural communication

The Star-to-Superstar Résumé

The following is a ready-to-use template for your college résumé. Simply replace the bracketed text with your own information and showcase your remarkable project.

[YOUR NAME]

[Your high school]

YOUR JOURNEY, FROM [STARTING POINT] TO [REMARKABLE ACHIEVEMENT]

[Start with something that captures your personal transformation—e.g., "From science enthusiast to published researcher"]

REMARKABLE PROJECT

[Project Name (Year–Year)]

— Problem identified: [Specific challenge you recognized]

— Solution created: [What you developed or initiated]

— Skills utilized: [Key abilities you applied or developed]

— Impact: [Concrete numbers of people affected, growth achieved, etc.]

— Recognition: [Any awards, publications, or other validation received]

— Evidence: [URL or other reference for proof of your accomplishment, if applicable]

PROGRESSION STORY

Initial Role/Activity (Year–Year)

— [Specific responsibility or achievement]

— [A skill developed or a lesson learned]

— [Early recognition, if applicable]

Growing Responsibility (Year–Year)

— [New skill learned or increased involvement]

— [Achievement showing personal growth]

— [Contribution to an organization/team]

Major Leadership Position (Year–Year)

— Led [specific group or initiative]

— Grew [specific improvement in project]

— Implemented [new program or approach]

Remarkable Achievement Project (Year–Year)

— Developed [specific aspect related to main project]

— Organized [event or initiative showing growth]

— Achieved [result building toward your remarkable project]

AWARDS & HONORS

12th Grade

— [Most prestigious award]

— [Recognition related to your remarkable project]

— [Any other significant honor]

11th Grade

— [Awards showing progression—Honorable Mention, 2nd Place]

— [Any subject-specific recognition]

10th Grade

— [Early achievements]

9th Grade

— [Foundational achievements—summer programs, first-level computer science, precollege program, etc.]

ACTIVITIES

Primary Activity Related to Your Remarkable Project (Year–Year)

— [Hours spent per week/weeks per year]

— [Growth or progression in your involvement]

— [Your specific contribution or achievement]

Secondary Activity (Year–Year)

— [Hours per week/weeks per year]

— [Leadership role, if applicable]

— [Personal achievement or contribution]

Community Service/Volunteer Work (Year–Year)

— [Hours per week/weeks per year]

— [Your specific contribution]

— [Your impact or achievement]

ADDITIONAL EXPERIENCES

Summer Program/Internship (Year)

— [Selective nature of program, e.g., "Selected from 500 applicants"]

— [Specific project or responsibility]

— [Achievement or skill developed]

Other Relevant Experience (Year)

— [Description of experience]

— [Relevance to your goals or "remarkable project"]

ACADEMIC PROFILE

— GPA: [weighted/unweighted]

— Test scores:
[SAT (including math, reading scores) / ACT]

— Relevant coursework: [Your most advanced or relevant courses]

— Languages: [Languages studied and proficiency levels]

— Technical skills: [Relevant technical abilities]

Formatting Tips:

— Use a consistent font throughout your application—11 or 12 point in a professional style such as Arial or Calibri.

— Maintain even spacing between sections.

— Use boldface section headings for easy scanning.

— Consider using some minimal color to highlight key elements (your name, section headings).

— Keep your résumé to one or two pages maximum.

— Save your document as a PDF to maintain the formatting.

— Attach this form to other forms you have to fill out regarding extracurricular activities.

CHAPTER 21

Getting Sticky Recommendations— Building Your Champions

*"The best time to plant
a tree was twenty years ago.
The second best time is now."*

—CHINESE PROVERB

ood recommendations can change the trajectory of your life. Take Jack, whom you met earlier (page 117). He's the one who had only a 3.1 GPA, struggled mightily in school after his father died of AIDS, and at the end of tenth grade thought he'd be headed for community college. But he's also the one who worked to bring his SATs up to 1540 and turned his life around in his last two years of high school, creating a successful DJ side business to help his mother financially and receiving an award from Haas Business School at UC Berkeley. But without teacher and counselor recommendations to attest not only to his turnaround but to his potential, Columbia would never have let him in. His stellar recommendations transformed his life.

This chapter is about how to get rave reviews from your recommenders. But first, let me share with you two recommendations I recently read so that you can easily see the difference between star and superstar rave reviews.

The first review was perfectly fine: "John is an excellent student who always turns in his work on time. He participates in class discussions and shows strong analytical skills. He will be successful in college."

The second started differently: "Congratulations! You just found one for the 'for sure' pile. Teresa is the best of the best, and I would have a hard time recommending anyone better. My recommendation is to save yourself some time, skip the rest of this letter, put it in the short stack, and keep up the good hunt."

Which student got into Yale? You already know the answer. Teresa's recommendation wasn't just positive—it was enthusiastically sticky. It made the reader care. It told a story. Most importantly, it validated what Teresa's application claimed about her being exceptional.

The Truth About Recommendations

Here's something most students don't understand: Your recommendations aren't just supporting documents, they're critical evidence that proves your story is real. When your essay claims that you're remarkable, your recommendations need to back that up.

Here are three key truths about recommendations:

1. They validate your transformation from star to superstar.

2. They prove that your remarkable project really made an impact.

3. They show that others believe in you and care about your success.

And here's the secret most students miss: You don't *find* great recommenders, you *develop* them. Think of it like growing a garden. You can't plant seeds the day before harvest and expect beautiful flowers. The same is true for recommendations. Here's a timeline for building champions to support you.

Freshman Year: Plant the Seeds

— Identify three or four teachers in core subjects and show genuine interest in their classes.

— Stay after class for help even when you don't desperately need it.

— Share outside interests that connect to their subjects.

Peter loved music, but he knew that he needed strong STEM recommendations for computer science. From day one in physics, he connected music and wave theory, asked about sound frequencies, and shared his orchestra experiences. This early connection laid the groundwork for his later iOS music app project.

Sophomore Year: Nurture Growth

— Take on leadership in your classes.

— Help other students.

— Start connecting classroom learning to outside projects.

— Keep teachers updated on your activities.

Angela knew that she wanted to be an English major. Instead of just being a good student, she started a peer tutoring program and shared her Scholastic Award submissions with her teacher. The result? Her teacher became a true champion for her creative writing dreams.

Junior Year: Deep Roots

— Ask for guidance on projects.

— Seek advice about summer programs.

— Share both successes and challenges with your teachers.

— Use your teachers' recommendations for summer programs.

Senior Year: Harvest Time

— By now, you should have two or three strong champions.

— They've witnessed your transformation.

— They're invested in your success.

— They're eager to write powerful recommendations.

If this timeline seems like a lot of work, here's a more direct route: Make two teachers your friends—friends who root for you, believe in you, and want you to succeed. Quite frankly, along with your essay, the difference between a great versus an average recommendation can make or break your chances for an Early Decision college.

Counselor Recommendation: Your Secret Opportunity

Here's a truth most students miss: Your counselor's recommendation can be just as powerful as a teacher's, even if they've barely met you. Why? Because counselors often have the last word on your character, resilience, and impact on the school community. Yet, in many public schools, counselors work with three hundred or more students, so they might not know you personally. But here's the secret: Their questionnaires (if they use them) are your chance to help them tell your story.

Making the Most of Counselor Questionnaires

Some high schools have a counselor's questionnaire, which they use as background for their counselor report. You need to respond to this questionnaire thoughtfully, going into depth and detail.

Wrong way (basic response): "Speech & Debate has been my main activity. I'm treasurer and participate in tournaments."

Right way (Alex's response): "Speech & Debate has given me the most joy because of how it transformed me. Growing up as an only child in a Chinese-speaking household, I was incredibly shy. But in eighth grade, something changed. At a town hall meeting, I spoke up against a local development project.

For the first time, I realized my voice mattered. This led me to join Speech & Debate, where I've grown from a nervous freshman to someone who helps other students find their voices."

See the difference? Alex's response

— shows transformation (shy kid to confident leader);

— provides specific context (comes from a Chinese-speaking household);

— gives concrete examples (stands up in a town hall meeting); and

— demonstrates impact on others (helping other students).

The Magic Document

One of the best ways to fill in a recommender's knowledge about you is to write a document called "Four Things You May Not Know About Me." When asking for a recommendation from someone, provide them with your résumé, a draft of your college essay if you have it, and these bits of information:

1. **Class impact.** "In your AP Biology class, I learned [a specific concept] that inspired me to [take a specific action]…"

2. **Outside growth.** "You may not know that I used what I learned about cellular biology to create a research project at a summer program…"

3. **Personal connection.** "Your encouragement when I struggled with [a specific challenge] helped me develop [something specific]…"

4. **Remarkable project.** "One thing you may not know about me is that for the last two years I have been developing an after-school project in…"

Making Recommendations Sticky

Remember how we've talked about sticky essays? The same principles apply here. Your recommendations need to

— tell a compelling story;

— make the reader care;

— provide evidence of your impact; and

— show your transformation.

Your recommendations should reinforce the center of your wheel (described on page 161). When your recommenders understand your center story, they can provide evidence that strengthens it rather than just listing random achievements.

How do you go about making that happen? By your connection to your recommenders—by giving them as much info as you can and by caring about them and their classes.

Here are some ways to keep relationships with your teachers strong.

— Quick updates (monthly): "Dear Ms. Chen, Just wanted to share that I used what I learned about hypothesis testing in your class for my science fair project. Thank you for making statistics so clear! I've attached a photo of my poster…"

— Meaningful connections (quarterly): "Hi Mr.

Rodriguez, Remember our discussion about [specific topic]? I just read an article that made me think of it…"

— Progress reports (per semester): "Dear Mrs. Williams, I wanted to update you on the tutoring program we discussed. We now have twelve students and…"

Bringing It All Together for Irresistible Recommendations

Here's the bottom line: When an admissions officer reads your recommendations, you want them to say, "We have to have this kid!" Not just "this is a good student," but "our university *needs* this student!"

Remember what I always say: You become eligible with your mind, but you get in with your heart. Your recommendations are where others confirm that your heart and your *character* are just as impressive as your transcript.

Think about what happened with Jack and his last-minute transformation that got him into Columbia. His math teacher didn't just write about his grades, but said, "Jack is in my calc class and has clearly become one of the top students. He started slow at math in ninth and tenth grades but has caught up now and is excelling." His history teacher didn't just write about his AP score, but said, "I have been teaching history and political science now for seventeen years. Jack, without a doubt, is proving himself to be one of the top students we have ever had (AP US History and Government)."

That's what makes recommendations irresistible—when teachers tell the story of a student who had this kind of impact:

— Takes initiative (like Linda building Speech & Debate from five to thirty members)

— Shows transformation (like Terry growing from a shy kid to a confident leader who did something politically for his community by campaigning for zoning)

— Creates lasting impact (like Selina's writing workshop that continued after she graduated)

— Revolutionizes how something is done (like Peter transforming the way his orchestra and others prepare for concerts)

Your job isn't just to get good recommendations; it's to become the kind of student others can't help but champion. Start early. Build genuine relationships. Do remarkable things. Keep your teachers and counselors informed. Make it easy for them to tell your remarkable story.

When your recommendations make admissions officers *feel* something—make them care about you and what you'll bring to their campus—that's when they'll fight for your acceptance.

CHAPTER 22

How to Do a Sticky College Interview

It's unusual for a student to call me directly, since most use text or email nowadays. So my interest was immediately piqued when Joseph called. Then, when the first thing he said was "You were right," I felt like I'd died and gone to heaven.

"How?" I croaked.

He answered, "My interview turned into a conversation, and I knew I had aced it."

Joseph had spent hours prepping his interview. He had answered all the questions in writing (you'll find them in this chapter), particularly those tricky open-ended ones such as "So tell me a little about yourself." He'd practiced answering them with me and with his dad. He'd brought his résumé so that his interviewer could look directly at it while asking questions.

And because he was overprepared, he was actually relaxed for the interview. Whether you do your interview online or at a neighborhood Starbucks, you need to be so well versed in your answers that at some point, hopefully, the interviewer drops the questions and becomes so interested in you that it turns into the give-and-take of a real conversation. Having a conversation instead of an interview doesn't always mean you've aced it, but it can be an indication. For Joseph, it was—he got into Brown with blue and white flying colors!

The Secret to Success: Making Them Care

Remember what we learned about sticky essays: You become eligible with your mind, but you get in with your heart. The same principle applies to college interviews. When your interviewers care about you, they become your champions in the admissions process.

How do you get them to care about you? You tell them an authentic, moving story.

Let me tell you about Linda, who interviewed at Pomona. Instead of just listing her achievements, she started by sharing how she'd transformed her school's dying Speech & Debate program. "When I became president," she said, "we had five members who mostly played games on their phones. Today, we have thirty active members competing at state level."

The interviewer leaned forward. "Tell me more about how you did that." Linda had made herself sticky. She got the interviewer to care. How do you do that? Here are three keys to a sticky interview:

1. **Position yourself before you walk in.** The interview is your opportunity to verbally express the center of your wheel and show how all your experiences connect to

that. When you position yourself clearly, interviewers can immediately see the coherence in your application. You need to walk in knowing exactly who you are in relationship to that college. That doesn't mean everything you've done—just what matters most to them.

Here's a quick exercise for you. Complete this sentence: "I am someone who…" This is your theme—what makes you uniquely valuable to this college. Here are some examples:

Weak: "I am someone who gets good grades and does lots of activities."

Strong: "I am someone who builds communities where none existed before."

2. **Tell stories, not lists.** Remember our sticky essay principle: Stories are what make people care. When your interviewer asks about leadership, don't just say you were club president. Tell them about the problem you faced, how you solved it, what changed because of you, and what you learned from that experience. Here are some examples:

Weak: "I was president of the Environmental Club."

Strong: "When I became president, our Environmental Club was just five kids picking up trash. I realized we needed to make environmental action more relevant to our high school. So we started an Instagram challenge that grew our membership to thirty students and led to a school-wide recycling program that reduced our waste by 40%."

3. **Make it about contribution, not achievement.** Here's something crucial that I've learned in thirty years of

coaching: Interviewers care less about what you've achieved and more about how you'll contribute to their community. So think about what you'll bring to campus, how you made your high school better, how you'll use that same energy to make your college better, what unique perspective you offer, and how you'll engage with others.

Weak: "I started our writing tutoring program, The Writer's Block."

Strong: "At my high school we had a peer math tutoring program that AP math students participated in for extra credit. But we had nothing like that for writing. So I formed a group of AP English students who convinced our teachers to give us extra credit if we helped younger students with their essays. Today we have 15 peer tutors who work with over 50 students twice a week at noon."

Your Sticky Interview Preparation

1. Know your own sticky story.

   — What experience best shows who you are?

   — Which story shows your impact on others?

   — What makes you different from other strong candidates?

2. Research deeply.

   — What makes this college unique?

   — How does your story match the college's values?

   — What specific programs excite you?

3. Prepare your "evidence."

   — What concrete examples prove your own impact? If you've got pictures, a website, or a video, show them!

   — What numbers show your personal growth?

   — What testimonials can back up your story?

Making Every Interview Answer Sticky

The first question—"Tell me about yourself"—is your chance to position yourself. Don't start with "I'm a junior at…" Instead, jump right into what makes you memorable. "Let me tell you about how I discovered my passion for bringing music to underserved communities…"

When the interviewer asks you about leadership

— don't just list positions you've held, tell a story about solving a real problem;

— show the ways you've inspired others; and

— share what you've learned about leading others.

When the interviewer asks you about your academic interests

— don't just name subjects, share what has sparked your curiosity;

— tell how you've pursued that interest; and

— connect this interest to college programs.

When the interviewer asks you about challenges

— don't focus on the difficulty you've encountered;

— show how you've grown and what you've learned; and

— connect that to how you'll contribute.

Key Interview Questions

1. "Tell me about yourself."

   Make it: "Let me share what really drives me…"

2. "Why our college?"

   Make it: "I've found three specific ways I feel that I could contribute here…"

3. "What's your greatest strength?"

   Make it: "Let me tell you about a time that shows my greatest strength…"

4. "Tell me about a challenge you've had."

   Make it: "Here's how I turned a problem into an opportunity…"

5. "What questions do you have?"

   Make it: "I'm curious about how I could contribute to…"

Your own questions reveal as much as your answers do. Ask the interviewer about

— how students collaborate;

— what makes the school's community special;

— how you could contribute; and

— what the interviewer loves about the school.

The Sticky Follow-Up

After your interview, send a thank-you note that

— references specific conversation points;

— reinforces your key story;

— adds any points you missed; and

— expresses genuine enthusiasm.

The Power of Simple Video Evidence

Some colleges request short videos in lieu of interviews as part of their application process, and this trend is growing. When my student Linda received this request from Pomona, she initially panicked. "I can't make one of those fancy videos I see on YouTube," she told me. "I don't know how to edit or add special effects."

What Linda didn't realize—and what most students miss—is that colleges aren't looking for production value. They're looking for evidence of your story and a glimpse of your authentic self.

Linda's video was remarkably simple, yet incredibly effective. She spoke directly to the camera, explaining how she had transformed her school's Speech & Debate Club. What made her video powerful wasn't fancy editing; it was the evidence she included:

— Four years of yearbook photos showing the club's growth from five to fifty students

— A brief clip of members practicing

— A simple photo shot across trophies they'd won

— The handbook she'd written for the club so that it could continue without her

Similarly, when Cynthia, who had a strong music background, applied to Northwestern's math department, she wanted them to be aware of her musical talent but didn't create an elaborate production. She simply spoke briefly about her journey as a violinist, had her medals and certificates on display around her, and included a thirty-second clip of her playing the violin. The admissions officer who interviewed Cynthia later told her that the video made her application "come alive" in a way her essay alone couldn't.

Your goal isn't to impress anyone with your video skills. Your goal is to provide evidence that makes your story believable and memorable. A simple, authentic video with concrete proof of your impact will always outperform a slick production that lacks substance.

Quick Tips for Effective Application Videos

— Speak naturally, as if talking to a friend.

— Include two or three pieces of physical evidence to support your story.

— Keep it simple; good lighting and clear sound matter more than special effects.

— Show, don't just tell; brief demonstrations are powerful.

— Be yourself! Authenticity resonates more than perfection.

Remember: It's about contribution, not about deserving acceptance. The goal isn't to impress with achievements or video skills; it's to make the interviewer care about having you on their campus. When you make yourself sticky, they'll want to champion your application.

Think of your interview as a conversation about how you made your high school better and how you'll bring that same initiative to the college—not just about why you deserve to get in. That's what makes an interview truly sticky.

As Joseph discovered, when you prepare thoroughly but stay authentic, the interview can transform into a genuine conversation. That's when you know you've succeeded in making yourself memorable—the interviewer stops thinking about the next question and starts thinking about how much you'd contribute to their campus.

Interview Preparation Worksheet

To prepare for your college interview, fill out the following worksheet:

1. "Center of the Wheel" statement:

   I am someone who (enjoys…cares about…made a difference by…): _______________

2. My remarkable story:

   A problem I identified: _______________

   How I addressed it: _______________

   The impact I made: _______________

   What I learned: _______________

3. How I'll contribute to [college name]:

   A specific program I'm excited about: _______________

   How I'll get involved: _______________

   What perspective I'll bring: _______________

4. My research notes on [college name]:

   Unique aspects of this college: _______________

   Values that align with mine: _______________

   Questions I want to ask: _______________

5. Practice answers to common interview questions:

   "Tell me about yourself." _______________

   "Why this college?" _______________

   "What's your greatest strength?" _______________

   "Describe a challenge you've faced." _______________

6. Follow-up plan:

   Key points to include in a thank-you note: _______________

Remember: Your goal is to be so well prepared that you can relax and let the conversation flow naturally. When your interviewer sees not just what you've done but who you are and how you'll contribute, that's when you'll truly stand out.

PART IV

Picking a Superstar College That Loves Your Story

Designing Your Future

Congratulations! You've reached what I consider the most exciting part of the college admissions journey. If you've been following the guidance in the previous chapters, you've already

— crafted a sticky essay that makes admissions officers care about you;

— created a remarkable project that demonstrates your initiative and impact; and

— built compelling evidence through honors, achievements, and strong recommendations.

In other words, you've become a superstar! And if you've followed the path outlined in these pages, you're not just applying to college—you're designing your future. Now it's time to find colleges that will truly appreciate your specific kind of excellence.

The Inverted Pyramid Approach

Most students approach college admissions backward. They start by identifying "dream schools" and then try to become the student those schools want. This puts all the power in the hands of admissions officers and leaves students scrambling to check boxes and pad their résumés.

I teach the opposite approach—what I call the inverted college pyramid.

First, become a superstar by

— following your genuine passions;

— creating remarkable projects that have real impact;

— building compelling evidence of your excellence; and

— developing a sticky story that makes people care.

Now find colleges that will appreciate your specific kind of excellence by

— understanding different college "personalities";

— identifying schools that value your particular strengths;

— matching your superstar qualities to the right institutions; and

— applying strategically to maximize your chances as an Asian American.

This approach gives you something precious: control. While you can't control who admits you, you *can* control the quality of your application and the strategic choices you make. The following three chapters will show you how to leverage your superstar qualities to maximize your chances of admission.

You'll learn all of the following:

— The dramatic advantage of Early Decision (often three or four times better odds)

— How your choice of a major can double or halve your chances

— Why bigger schools can mean better odds for Asian American students

— How to match your personality to colleges that will truly "get" you

— Why the same application can read completely differently from one school to another

— How to build a balanced list of colleges that maximizes your chances

— The importance of finding schools that will value your remarkable project

This is where all the pieces come together. Your superstar qualities aren't just about getting in somewhere; they're about finding where you'll truly belong and thrive.

Remember: The college admissions process isn't a judgment of your worth. It's a matching process, pairing students with institutions where they'll succeed. Your job isn't just to be "good enough" to get in, it's to find colleges where your specific kind of excellence will be celebrated, not merely tolerated.

Let's begin designing your future!

CHAPTER 24

The College Personality Match

Where you go is not who you'll be. But who you are will determine where you should go.

—ADAPTED FROM FRANK BRUNI

A few years ago I met with George, a talented student with a 4.0 GPA and a 1520 SAT score. His parents were convinced that Stanford was the perfect fit, pointing to his impressive accomplishments—president of his school's coding club, creator of a helpful academic app, winner of regional hackathons. "He's done everything right," they insisted.

But here's what they didn't understand: At Stanford, George would be competing against students who'd not only started coding clubs but had created educational platforms used by thousands across multiple countries. His achievements, while excellent, made him a star—but not necessarily a Stanford superstar.

When we shifted our focus to colleges that would truly value his specific kind of excellence, George applied for Early Decision at Carnegie Mellon University. The secret advantage? Carnegie Mellon's personality perfectly matched his strengths. George wasn't just a coder, but a musician who'd played flute since age seven and was in two orchestras. CMU's unique appreciation for students who bridge technology and the arts made his application shine, whereas elsewhere it might have been overlooked.

George thrived at Carnegie Mellon, leading research projects that combined music and technology and also mentoring other students. He'd found a college that matched not just his academic credentials, but his unique personality. This is what happens when you become a superstar first, then find schools that truly "get" you.

The College Personality Framework

Think of colleges the way you think of people: Each one has its own distinct personality, values, and quirks. After decades of helping students navigate the admissions process, I've identified distinct "personality types" among elite institutions. Understanding these different personalities is crucial to finding your own perfect match.

For intellectual mavericks:

🎯 University of Chicago

- Loves quirky intellectuals, unconventional thinkers

- Famous for its motto "Life of the Mind," where intellectual engagement is central to everyday life and thought-provoking yet amusing application essays

- Perfect for students who write essays comparing quantum physics to the work of David Foster Wallace

- Sticky sweet spot: deep thinkers who don't take themselves too seriously

For Renaissance scholars:

🎯 Columbia University

- Loves synthesizers who connect different disciplines

- Famous for its core curriculum—everyone reads the "Great Books"

- Perfect for students who see connections between AI, philosophy, and physics

- Sticky sweet spot: deep readers who can connect ideas across fields

For purposeful innovators:

🎯 Stanford University

- Loves students who "make things" and create scalable impact with them

- Famous for its "change the world" entrepreneurial spirit

- Perfect for dreamers who actually build their dreams

- Sticky sweet spot: combining excellence with real-world impact

For engaged citizens:

🎯 Yale University

- Loves community builders and cultural connectors

- Famous for its residential college system and emphasis on collaboration

- Perfect for leaders who lift others as they rise

- Sticky sweet spot: excellence with genuine humility and service

For independent thinkers:

🎯 Brown University

- Loves self-directed learners who create their own paths

- Famous for its open curriculum, in which students design their own education

- Perfect for students who purposefully color outside the lines

- Sticky sweet spot: academic excellence with creative independence

For scholarly leaders:

🎯 Princeton University

- Loves deep thinkers who lead by example

- Famous for its senior thesis requirement, for which everyone does original research

- Perfect for students who dive deep while reaching wide

- Sticky sweet spot: intellectual rigor plus practical leadership

For professional innovators:

🎯 University of Pennsylvania (Penn)

- Loves students who bridge theory and practice

- Famous for combining liberal arts with pre-professional focus—finance, medicine, engineering

- Perfect for future leaders who want broad *and* deep impact

- Sticky sweet spot: academic excellence with practical application

Why One Size Doesn't Fit All

To understand why it matters that you match your personality to a college, let's look at how the same student profile can read completely differently at various institutions.

The tech leader—Jennifer's story:

— 4.0 GPA, 1580 SAT score

— Created an AI app analyzing music patterns

— Led coding workshops for middle school girls

— Played violin in youth symphony

— Started a tech-music fusion club

— Published research on music pattern recognition

How different schools might see her:

🎯 MIT (Massachusetts Institute of Technology)

- Perfect fit! Jennifer builds things that matter and bridges technology with human experience.

- Her coding workshops show she can teach and lead.

- Likely outcome: Strong accept

🎯 Stanford University

- Good but not groundbreaking. App is interesting, but for whom? What's the scalable impact? Local workshops are nice, but where's the wider influence?

- Likely outcome: Probable reject

🎯 Northwestern University

- Love this fusion of arts and technology! Exactly the cross-disciplinary innovation we value.

- Likely outcome: Strong consider

🎯 Duke University

- Strong academics but impact feels narrow. Where's the community building beyond tech circles?

- Likely outcome: Possible reject

The final outcome? Jennifer got into MIT.

The community changemaker—Terry's story:

— 3.9 GPA, 1520 SAT score

— Founded a nonprofit teaching debate to immigrant

students as a way to develop both English and debating skills

— Created a translation service for immigrant parent-teacher conferences

— Won state debate championships

— Published articles about immigrant education

— Started his school's first Asian-Latino Alliance

How different schools might see him:

🎯 Yale University

- Terry is perfect Yale material! Builds community, crosses cultural boundaries, shows leadership with genuine impact.

- Likely outcome: Strong accept

🎯 Columbia University

- Interesting bridge-builder, but where's the intellectual depth? Community work is impressive but looking for more analytical rigor.

- Likely outcome: Possible reject

🎯 Duke University

- Love the Southern hospitality meets global perspective Terry brings. Strong community impact with measurable results.

- Likely outcome: Strong consider

🎯 University of Pennsylvania (Penn)

- Good leadership, but where's the scalable model? Looking for more entrepreneurial approach to social change.

- Likely outcome: Probable reject

The final outcome? Terry got into Yale.

The Inverted Pyramid Approach

Most students follow a traditional approach—they identify target schools first, then try to become the student those schools want. But I teach my students to invert this process through the following steps.

1. Become a superstar first by checking all these boxes:

    — Developing your genuine passions

    — Creating remarkable projects

    — Writing sticky essays

    — Building compelling evidence

2. Then find colleges that appreciate your specific kind of excellence. This "inverted pyramid" approach gives you something precious: the ability to direct your situation. While you can't control who admits you, here's what you *can* direct:

    — The quality of your remarkable project

    — The stickiness of your essays

    — The strategic choices in your college list

    — Where you apply for Early Decision

Here's a quick exercise to help you start identifying colleges that match your personality: Circle the statements that feel true for you:

— "I love learning for learning's sake." (Chicago)

— "I see connections across different subjects." (Columbia)

— "I want to create scalable, real-world impact." (Stanford)

— "I build community wherever I go." (Yale)

— "I create my own unique path." (Brown)

— "I dive deep while reaching wide." (Princeton)

— "I turn ideas into action." (Penn)

For each statement you circled, research the corresponding school and at least two similar institutions. Look beyond the obvious Ivy League schools—many excellent institutions share the same personality traits.

The Secret: It's Not About Being "Good Enough"

Remember Olivia from earlier chapters? With her 1500 SAT score, writing achievements, and literary magazine for immigrant voices, she was rejected from Harvard but thrived at Wesleyan. Why? Not because she wasn't "good enough" for Harvard, but because Wesleyan's personality—valuing creative expression, social awareness, and intimate community impact—perfectly matched her own strengths.

At Wesleyan, Olivia's writing achievements weren't just admissions credentials; they were celebrated as the start of a promising literary career. Her immigrant voices project wasn't just another activity; it was exactly the kind of initiative Wesleyan values. Success isn't about getting into the highest-ranked school. Success is finding a school where your kind of excellence isn't just accepted but is celebrated— a place where you can truly thrive.

As we move into more strategic considerations for building your college list, remember this fundamental truth: The college admissions process isn't just about getting in somewhere; it's about finding where *you* belong!

By now, if you've followed the guidance in the previous chapters, you're already a superstar with a sticky essay that makes people care, a remarkable project that demonstrates your initiative, and evidence and recommendations to back up your excellence. The next step isn't about becoming "better"—it's about finding schools that will truly value your specific kind of excellence. That's where the real magic happens.

Let's get tactical about creating a balanced college list that maximizes your chances of admission while ensuring that you'll thrive wherever you go.

Building Your Strategic College List

Now that you're a superstar with a compelling story, a remarkable project, and evidence to back it all up, it's time to design your future by choosing colleges that will truly value what you bring to the table. This is where all your hard work pays off—where you transform your superstar qualities into strategic college choices.

Working with thousands of students over the decades, I've seen this pattern repeatedly: The most successful college outcomes don't come from chasing prestige blindly, but from making strategic choices based on understanding how each institution will read your application. In fact, the best college for you isn't necessarily the most prestigious one that accepts you; it's the one where your specific kind of excellence will be most valued and nurtured.

Let me share a real example that shows how this works. Olivia (page 31) was an excellent student with a clear passion for writing and English literature. Unlike many of her Asian American peers who struggled through

AP Calculus BC courses to check a box, Olivia made a strategic choice: She decided to take less advanced math courses instead, focusing her energy on what genuinely energized her. Her SATs reflected this strategic approach: 780 reading, 675 math. Not perfect, but perfectly aligned with her strengths. She became editor in chief of her school's literary magazine, won scholastic writing awards, and got into competitive creative writing programs at California State Summer School for the Arts, Kenyon College, and the University of Iowa.

When it came time to build her college list, Olivia didn't chase the highest-ranked schools. Instead, she looked for colleges that would value her specific kind of excellence. She applied for Early Decision to Wesleyan University— a school known for valuing exactly her combination of talents—as an English major with a creative writing minor. The result? Early Decision acceptance to a top university where her strengths would be celebrated, not merely tolerated.

Olivia's success wasn't about being "perfect at everything." It was about being exceptional at something and finding a college that valued that exceptionality.

Here's the key insight: These categories aren't just about a school's overall acceptance rate. They're about how *your* specific profile will be read at *that* specific institution.

The Dream College Funnel & Bottleneck

Think of your college search as a funnel, starting broad and then narrowing to your perfect matches. Here's how to narrow down your choices.

The Dream College Funnel & Bottleneck

ALL STUDENTS

STEP 1:
BASIC INFO

- School Size
- Location
- Program Offerings
- Campus Culture

STEP 2:
ACADEMIC FIT

- Meet GPA/SAT Requirements
- Course Rigor
- Major Match

STEP 3:
REALITY CHECK

- Overall Acceptance Rate
- Demographic Acceptance Rate
- Major acceptance rate
- Regular vs Early Decision%

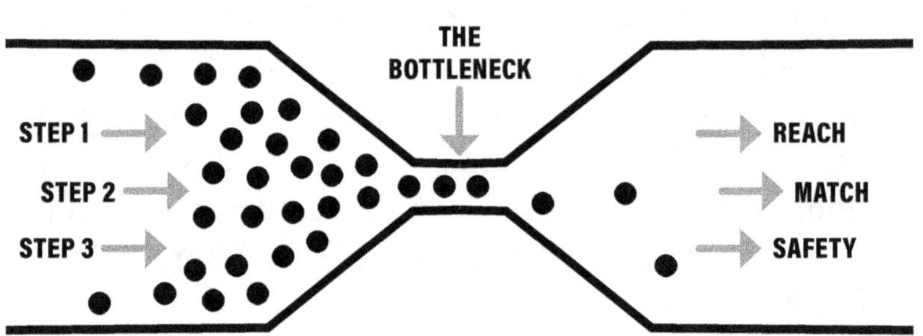

ASIAN-AMERICAN STUDENTS

THE BOTTLENECK

- Like Cancels Like (Asians Compete Against Other Asians)
- They Compete for the Same Majors (Engineering, Computer Science, Business)

BREAKING THE BOTTLENECK

- **STRATEGY 1–** strategic school selection
- **STRATEGY 2–** alternative major paths

FINAL COLLEGE LIST

- Reach
- Match
- Safety

(Include % of overall admit, % of Asian admit using breaking the bottleneck strategies)

STEP 1: BASIC INFORMATION. Begin by asking yourself some simple but crucial questions:

— What size school will help you thrive, from 1,100 students at Pomona to 73,000+ at Texas A&M?

— What are your geographic preferences—region, urban, or rural, and how far from home?

— What academic programs are in your field of interest?

— What is the campus culture and environment?

STEP 2: ACADEMIC MATCH. Consider these factors:

— Does the school offer your intended major/program?

— How strong is their department in your field?

— Do you meet their GPA and test score ranges for acceptance?

— Will they value your choices of difficult high school courses?

STEP 3: DEMOGRAPHIC REALITY CHECK. This is where many Asian American students stumble and why it's important to understand the following:

— What is the school's overall acceptance rate?

— What is the acceptance rate for your demographic group?

— What is the acceptance rate for your intended major?

— What is the school's Early Decision/Action advantage?

Let's look at some real numbers that illustrate this reality.

Cornell University (2023 data)

— Overall acceptance rate: 10.7%

— Asian American enrollment: 20% (of 10.7%)

— Early Decision advantage: 24% versus 8.7% for regular application

— School-specific acceptance differences: Engineering 5.2%, Arts & Sciences 11%, Hotel School 30%

University of Pennsylvania (2023 data)

— Overall acceptance rate: 4.1%

— Asian American enrollment: 22% (of 4.1%)

— Early Decision advantage: 15.6% versus under 4% for regular application

— Program differences:

    ✦ Wharton School: Lower rate of acceptance

    ✦ Nursing School: Higher rate of acceptance

All these numbers reveal something crucial: Your chances vary dramatically depending on when you apply and what program you apply for—even at the same institution.[7]

---

7. Cornell University, "Common Data Set 2023–2024," Cornell University Institutional Research and Planning, 2023; University of Pennsylvania, "Common Data Set 2023–2024," Penn Institutional Research and Analysis, 2023.

The Bottleneck Problem

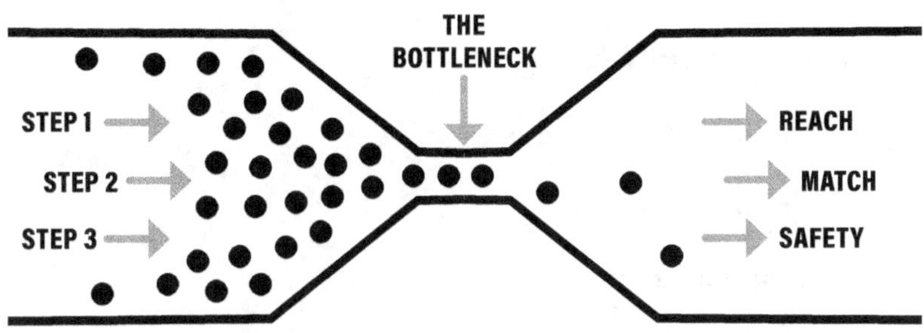

Here's a brutal truth that many counselors won't tell you: As an Asian American student, you face a "like cancels like" problem that's compounded with certain choices of majors. The bottleneck occurs when Asian American students compete within demographic quotas (as revealed in the Harvard 2018 lawsuit on Asian American bias—see Appendix 1, page 290) or when they choose the same handful of majors (like premed/biology, computer science, engineering, or business).

This creates intense competition within your demographic group. I've seen students with perfect GPAs and test scores rejected from top schools because they were indistinguishable from thousands of other Asian American applicants. But here are two powerful strategies for breaking through this bottleneck:

STRATEGY 1: ALTERNATIVE MAJOR PATHS. Consider these alternatives to standard majors.

Instead of premed/biology:

— Medical anthropology

— Public health

— Biomedical engineering

— Health psychology

— Global health

Instead of computer science:

— Human-computer interaction

— Digital media design

— Cognitive science

— Information systems

— Interactive media arts

Instead of engineering:

— Engineering physics

— Engineering psychology

— Environmental engineering

— Industrial design

— Engineering and public policy

Instead of business:

— Social entrepreneurship

— International development

— Design strategy

— Technology management

— Environmental economics

STRATEGY 2: STRATEGIC SCHOOL SELECTION.
In your search for the right school, look for the following:

— Schools with higher Asian American enrollment
(such as Caltech, at 40%)[8]

— Institutions with unique interdisciplinary programs

— Colleges known for valuing your specific
combination of interests

— Places where your remarkable project aligns with
institutional priorities

Where can you find such schools?

Here are a few suggestions:

— *Fiske Guide to Colleges*

— The Princeton Review's *The Best 390 Colleges* (2025)

— Donald Asher's *Cool Colleges*

— Loren Pope's *Looking Beyond the Ivy League*

---

8. California Institute of Technology, "Undergraduate Admission Statistics," Caltech
Office of Undergraduate Admissions, 2024.

Lane's Story: From Dream to Reality

Lane had been dreaming about Penn since his sophomore year. He'd visited campus twice, imagining himself walking Locust Walk, and picturing every detail of studying data science in the shadow of that prestigious Ivy League brand. Penn was the school. When he came to my office to talk about Early Decision strategy, he was ready to put all his eggs in the Penn basket.

"Let's run through the checklist first," I suggested.

Lane humored me. He had a 1530 SAT, a 3.95 GPA, and had completed every Golden 20 course. Lane built an AI tool that helps low-income families in his community find affordable housing by predicting rent increases six months in advance. He partnered with a local nonprofit that now uses his tool to help 200+ families annually avoid displacement. Furthermore, he was working with them to expand it to three neighboring counties. On paper, Lane was very competitive.

Then we looked at the numbers—really looked at them.

Penn accepted 4.1% of applicants overall. But when you factored in the 22% Asian American enrollment cap, the math became brutal: out of 44,961 applicants, only about 406 Asian students were admitted. That's 0.9%. Even with Early Decision's advantage, Lane was competing with thousands of high-achieving Asian American students for data science slots at Wharton or SEAS (School of Engineering and Applied Science)—precisely where everyone else with his profile was applying.

I pulled up Cornell's data. The overall acceptance rate was higher at 10.7%, and while Cornell's Asian American enrollment was slightly lower at 20%, they admitted far more students overall—1,066 Asian students from a larger applicant pool. More importantly, Cornell had seven different undergraduate colleges, each with its own acceptance rate. Lane could apply to data science, but he could also position himself through Statistics in Arts & Sciences or Information Science—pathways that faced less bottleneck pressure than direct computer science admits.

The Early Decision advantage at Cornell was substantial: 24% versus 8.7% regular decision. That was real leverage.

Lane stared at both spreadsheets. His dream school had a 0.9% acceptance rate for students who looked exactly like him, applying to exactly the programs everyone else chose. Cornell offered multiple entry points, a 24% ED acceptance rate, and admitted more than twice as many Asian students overall.

The choice was clear, even if it stung a little.

Lane applied Early Decision to Cornell's College of Arts & Sciences, expressing interest in their Statistics and Data Science major. He highlighted his machine learning project and positioned himself as someone interested in the intersection of data, social science, and policy—a less saturated lane than pure computer science.

In December, he got his acceptance letter.

Looking back, Lane realized something important: His dream hadn't really been about Penn specifically. It had been about getting an Ivy League education where he could thrive in data science. Cornell gave him that—and by working through the checklist, by understanding the bottleneck, and by choosing strategically, he'd turned a nearly impossible dream into reality.

Lane's College Comparison: Penn vs. Cornell

STEP 1: Basic Information

	U. OF PENNSYLVANIA	CORNELL UNIVERSITY
School Size	10,000+ undergrads	15,000+ undergrads
Location	Philadelphia, urban	Ithaca, college town
Program Offerings	Data Science program	Data Science, Statistics, Information Science across multiple colleges
Campus Culture	Pre-professional, competitive	Collaborative, multiple college cultures

STEP 2: Academic Fit

	U. OF PENNSYLVANIA	CORNELL UNIVERSITY
Major Match	Yes—Data Science	Yes—Multiple data science pathways
Department Strength	Strong, housed in Wharton/SEAS	Strong across Engineering, A&S, Computing & Info Science
Meet GPA/SAT Requirements	Yes (1530 SAT, 3.95 GPA)	Yes (1530 SAT, 3.95 GPA)
Course Rigor Valued	Yes—Golden 20 completed	Yes—Golden 20 completed

STEP 3: Reality Check

	U. OF PENNSYLVANIA	CORNELL UNIVERSITY
Overall Acceptance Rate	4.1% (Class of 2027)	10.7% (2023)
Total Applicants	44,961	49,114
Total Accepted	~1,844	5,330
Asian American Enrollment	22%	20%

Asian Students Accepted	~406 Asians	~1,066 Asians
Asian Acceptance Reality	0.9% of Asian applicants	2.2% of Asian applicants
Early Decision Advantage	15.6% ED vs. 4% RD	24% ED vs. 8.7% RD
ED Asian Acceptance (est.)	~176 students	~280 students

The Bottleneck

	U. OF PENNSYLVANIA	CORNELL UNIVERSITY
Like Cancels Like	Severe—competing against high-achieving Asians for data science/Wharton	Moderate—7 different colleges dilute competition
Same Major Competition	Intense—Data Science is impacted	Options—can apply to less competitive college (A&S, Statistics, Information Science)

Breaking the Bottleneck

	U. OF PENNSYLVANIA	CORNELL UNIVERSITY
STRATEGY 1: Strategic School Selection	Not optimal—extremely low Asian admit rate	Better—higher overall acceptance, multiple entry points
STRATEGY 2: Alternative Major Paths	Limited—Data Science is direct competition	Multiple—Statistics (A&S), Information Science, Computer Science (different colleges)

Lane's Rating

	U. OF PENNSYLVANIA	CORNELL UNIVERSITY
REACH	Nearly Impossible	Possible with ED

To break your own bottleneck, this table is available at the end of this chapter.

Understanding the Three College Categories

Before we dive into building your list, let's clarify what's meant by "reach, target, and safety" schools. These categories are more nuanced than many students realize.

Reach schools (less than 20% chance of admission) are places where your profile is strong but admission isn't guaranteed.

— They often include schools with acceptance rates of less than 15%.

— They may include slightly less selective schools if in a highly competitive demographic area.

— You may meet their academic bar but stand out less in their applicant pool.

Examples: Ivy League and Ivy Plus schools like Stanford, U of Chicago, UC Berkeley

Target schools (25–50% chance of admission) are places where your profile aligns well with typical admits.

— Your achievements stand out in their applicant pool.

— You're above average for admitted students.

— Admission is still not guaranteed, but you have a reasonable shot.

Examples: NYU, U of Michigan, Northeastern, Boston University

Safety or backup schools (greater than 50% chance of admission) are places where you're significantly above the typical admits.

— Similar students are routinely accepted.

— Your superstar qualities would make you a standout.

— You'd be happy to attend one of these schools if other options don't materialize.

Examples: Purdue, Fordham, U of Washington

Building Your Balanced List

Now let's get tactical about creating your college list. The exact distribution of schools to apply to may depend on whether you're a star or a superstar, but in either case, a balanced approach is needed.

Stars (strong students):

— Two or three reach schools

— Three or four target schools

— Two or three safety schools

Superstars (exceptional students):

— Four or five reach schools

— Two or three target schools

— One or two safety schools

Why not all "reach" schools? Because even superstars need options. The admissions process contains enough randomness that even perfect applications can get rejected. A balanced list ensures that you'll have choices come April.

Strategic college list template. For each school on your list, complete the following analysis.

Basic information:

— College name

— Size

— Location

— Why I'm interested

Academic fit:

— Program strength in my intended major

— Special opportunities in my field

— Faculty doing research I'm interested in

Admissions data:

— Average SAT/ACT test scores for admitted students (*Google or Perplexity search*)

— Overall acceptance rate

— Early Decision/Early Action acceptance rates

— Acceptance rate for my demographic (if available)

— Acceptance rate for my intended major/school (if available)

College values and priorities:

— Key institutional values (found in overview, mission statement, motto)

— Unique programs or opportunities

— How my remarkable project aligns with the school's focus

Personal fit assessment:

— Am I a star candidate at this school? A superstar candidate?

— Do I offer a compelling story that they'll value?

Final analysis:

— Classification of school (reach/target/safety)

— Application strategy (ED/EA/regular)

— Similar colleges to consider

— Next steps in researching the school

Major Strategy Assessment

Let's determine whether your current choice of a major might create a bottleneck.

1. Are you applying for one of these?

— Premed/biology

— Computer science

— Engineering

— Business

2. Are you Asian American?

3. Are your target schools highly selective (under 15% acceptance rate)?

If you answered "yes" to all three questions, consider the following:

- — What alternative majors might align with your interests?

- — Which schools have unique programs that combine your interests?

- — How can you position your remarkable project to stand out in your field?

This isn't about abandoning your interests; it's about finding a less crowded path to the same destination. Let me share a few success stories about students who broke through the bottleneck.

MICHELLE—FROM PREMED TO MEDICAL ANTHROPOLOGY. Michelle wanted to be a doctor, but recognized the premed bottleneck. She applied to Johns Hopkins as a medical anthropology major, highlighting her project of creating health education programs for immigrant communities. This unique angle positioned her differently from thousands of traditional premed applicants.

Result: Acceptance to Johns Hopkins, where she continued premed requirements while pursuing her interest in cultural approaches to medicine.

JASON—FROM COMPUTER SCIENCE TO DIGITAL MEDIA DESIGN. Jason loved coding but knew that computer science was ultracompetitive for Asian American males. He applied to Penn's Digital Media Design program, showcasing his remarkable project that combined coding with visual arts to create accessible tech tools for children with autism.

Result: Acceptance to Penn's DMD program with an interdisciplinary major in the School of Engineering and Applied Science, which taught him core computer science skills while distinguishing him from the mainstream computer science applicant pool.

KIARA—FROM BUSINESS TO ENVIRONMENTAL ECONOMICS. Kiara was passionate about business but wary of the competitive Wharton applicant pool. So she applied to Cornell's Environmental Economics program, highlighting her remarkable project of creating a sustainable recycling business in her community.

Result: Acceptance to Cornell, where she gained business foundations while positioning herself uniquely in the environmental sector.

Final Thoughts: Be Strategic, Not Deceptive

To be clear, this strategic approach isn't about being deceptive or abandoning your interests. It's about finding less congested paths to your goals and positioning yourself where your specific excellence will shine.

By now, you should understand

— the importance of building a balanced list
of colleges;

— how to assess schools beyond simple acceptance rates;

— the impact of demographic realities and your
choice of a major; and

— how to break through bottlenecks with strategic
positioning.

The Dream College Comparison Sheet

STEP 1: Basic Information

	COLLEGE #1	COLLEGE #2
School Size		
Location		
Program Offerings		
Campus Culture		

STEP 2: Academic Fit

	COLLEGE #1	COLLEGE #2
Major Match		
Department Strength		
Meet GPA/SAT Requirements		
Course Rigor Valued		

STEP 3: Reality Check

	COLLEGE #1	COLLEGE #2
Overall Acceptance Rate		
Total Applicants		
Total Accepted		
Asian American Enrollment		
Asian Students Accepted		
Asian Acceptance Reality		
Early Decision Advantage		
ED Asian Acceptance (est.)		

The Bottleneck

	COLLEGE #1	COLLEGE #2
Like Cancels Like		
Same Major Competition		

Breaking the Bottleneck

	COLLEGE #1	COLLEGE #2
STRATEGY 1: Strategic School Selection		
STRATEGY 2: Alternative Major Paths		

In the next chapter, we'll explore perhaps the most powerful strategic advantage available to you: the Early Decision option. This single choice can potentially triple or quadruple your odds of acceptance at your dream school!

Rating

	COLLEGE #1	COLLEGE #2
REACH		

CHAPTER 26

The Early Decision Advantage

I genuinely believe that Early Decision isn't just another option—it's the single most powerful strategic tool available to maximize your chances of being accepted at your dream school.

When Alex applied to Vanderbilt through Early Decision, he was rejected. That was a crushing moment, certainly, but not the end of his story. Because Alex had followed my guidance to develop superstar qualities, he had a backup plan. He applied to the University of Chicago through Early Decision II, showcasing his remarkable project and (quirky) sticky essay, and he was accepted.

The numbers don't lie. Early Decision can double, triple, or even quadruple your chances of admission. This chapter shows exactly how to use this powerful tool strategically, especially as an Asian American student facing the additional hurdles discussed throughout this book.

Understanding Your Options

Let's start by clarifying the various early application options available to you.

Early Decision (ED)

— Binding commitment: If accepted, you must attend.

— Deadline: Usually November 1

— Decision: Mid-December

— Advantage: Significantly higher acceptance rates (often two to four times higher than Regular Decision rates)

Early Decision II (ED II)

— Binding commitment: If accepted, you must attend.

— Deadline: Usually January 1

— Decision: Mid-February

— Advantage: Still higher acceptance rates than Regular Decision, though sometimes slightly lower than ED I

Restricted Early Action (REA) / Single-Choice Early Action (SCEA)

— Nonbinding: You can choose not to attend even if accepted.

— Restriction: You cannot apply early to other private schools.

— Deadline: Usually November 1

— Decision: Mid-December

— Advantage: Modest improvement in acceptance rates in the case of Stanford

Early Action (EA)

— Nonbinding: You can choose not to attend even if accepted.

— Deadline: Usually November 1

— Decision: Mid-December

— Advantage: Minimal or no statistical advantage in acceptance rates

Numbers Don't Lie: The ED Advantage

The advantage of applying for Early Decision is staggering, particularly at selective institutions. Let's look at real acceptance data from the class of 2027.

Acceptance Rates[9]

SCHOOL	REGULAR DECISION	EARLY DECISION	ED ADVANTAGE
Cornell	8.7%	24%	2.8x better odds
UPenn	3.5%	15.6%	3.9x better odds
Duke	4.4%	16.5%	3.7x better odds
Northwestern	5.2%	20.3%	3.9x better odds
Dartmouth	4.7%	19%	4.0x better odds

9. Based on institutional Common Data Sets and admissions reports: Cornell University (2023), University of Pennsylvania (2023), Duke University (2023), Northwestern University (2023), Dartmouth College (2023).

These aren't small differences—they're game changers! Applying for ED can turn a "reach" school into a "target," or a likely rejection into a probable acceptance.

The Hard Truth About Early Action

Here's an uncomfortable truth: Early Action—the nonbinding option—typically offers little to no advantage for Asian American students applying to elite institutions. While Early Action shows modest overall advantage at some schools, the benefit often disappears for Asian American applicants. Why is this so?

— Institutional priorities: Early Decision, as opposed to Early Action, brings committed students who will definitely attend the school, improving the yield rates.

— Demographic considerations: Schools often use EA to accept underrepresented minorities and legacy applicants.

— Demonstrated interest: EA doesn't show the same level of commitment that ED does.

As an example, Harvard's overall Early Action acceptance rate is higher than that for Regular Decision. But when broken down by demographic, the advantage for nonrecruited Asian American students is negligible. The EA pool is filled with recruited athletes, legacies, and other priority groups, leaving little room for "standard" Asian American applicants.

The bottom line? EA applications can feel good, because you might get an early acceptance somewhere. But if you're a nonlegacy, nonrecruited Asian American student, this "somewhere" is rarely going to be a highly selective institution that would have rejected you in the regular round. Don't waste your early card on EA if ED is an option.

The Financial Aid Question

The most common concern about Early Decision is financial aid: "What if I get in but can't afford it?" Here's what you need to know:

1. Most ED schools have a policy that releases you from your binding commitment if the financial aid package is genuinely inadequate.

2. Net price calculators (available on every college website) can give you a solid cost estimate before you apply.

3. Many schools that offer ED are actually committed to meeting 100% of demonstrated financial need (Google or use Perplexity to find out ahead of time).

If finances are a serious concern, here are some steps you can take:

— Use net price calculators on college websites before applying for ED.

— Contact school financial aid offices directly with your questions.

— Consider ED II at schools with strong financial aid histories.

— Look into ED schools with "no-loan" financial aid policies.

Don't let financial concerns automatically rule out ED—that would be taking your most powerful admission advantage off the table.

Strategic ED Decision-Making

Now that you understand the significant advantage of Early Decision, let's talk about how to choose where to apply. This isn't a decision to make lightly—it's potentially the most important strategic choice in your application process.

Step 1: Assess your competitiveness. Review your profile honestly:

— Are you a star or a superstar? (Review the assessment in the previous chapters.)

— How strong are you compared to typical admits? (Search YouTube, Reddit, and college discussions by students.)

— Does your "remarkable project" align with the school's values?

— Do your essays and recommendations strongly support your case?

Step 2: Research ED acceptance patterns. For each potential ED school, research the following:

— What is the overall ED acceptance rate?

— What is the ED advantage compared to Regular Decision?

— What percentage of the class is filled through ED?

— What are the success patterns for your demographic group? (Asian and Indian specifically)

Step 3: Consider your priorities. Ask yourself these questions:

— Is this truly my first-choice school?

— Would I be happy attending if accepted?

— Does this school value my specific kind of excellence?

— Am I comfortable with the binding commitment?

Step 4: Plan your ED/ED II strategy. Consider the following approaches:

Strategy A—Aim high, with backup:

— Apply to your realistic dream school with ED.

— If rejected, apply with ED II to another excellent option.

Example: Alex's Vanderbilt → Chicago path (page 251)

Strategy B—Choose certainty:

— Apply with ED to a school where you're a strong candidate.

— Prioritize a high probability of acceptance over a school's prestige.

Example: Olivia's Wesleyan ED choice (page 228) over Harvard REA (Restrictive Early Action)

Strategy C—Target program-specific advantages:

— Apply with ED to a school that has unusually high acceptance rates in your program.

Example: Cornell's School of Hotel Administration (30% versus 10.7% overall acceptance rate)[10]

---

10. Cornell University, "School of Hotel Administration Admission Statistics," Cornell University Common Data Set 2023–2024.

Case Studies: ED Success Stories

LEO—BREAKING THE ASIAN COMPUTER SCIENCE BOTTLENECK. Leo was a strong student (4.0 GPA, 1530 SAT score) who was interested in computer science. Rather than applying to Stanford or MIT along with thousands of similar applicants, he applied through ED to Brown University, emphasizing

— his remarkable project establishing a boys' high school tennis team;

— his combining of computer science with tennis when he created a more accessible competition tennis ladder website for teams in his district;

— his interest in Brown's open curriculum, paralleling his interest in literature, computer science, and athletics; and

— his ability to contribute to Brown's collaborative culture.

Result: Leo was accepted through ED at Brown, where he could pursue computer science in a less cutthroat environment.

PRIYA—USING ED II AFTER A DEFERRAL. Priya applied via EA to Yale (her absolute dream school) and was deferred to Regular Decision. Instead of hoping for a regular acceptance—with slim odds—she

— quickly evaluated her other top choices;

— applied through ED II to Vanderbilt; and

— tailored her application to showcase her interest in their specific programs.

Result: Priya was accepted through ED II at Vanderbilt, where she ultimately thrived.

The Financial Aid Strategy

Kamal came from a family with financial constraints, but he had strong credentials. Instead of avoiding ED, he

— used net price calculators to identify affordable options;

— applied through ED to Bowdoin College in Maine, known for generous financial aid; and

— highlighted how his remarkable project on the environment aligned with Bowdoin's values.

Result: Kamal was accepted through ED at Bowdoin with a strong financial aid package that made the school affordable for him.

Your ED Strategy Worksheet

Complete this worksheet to determine your best ED approach.

Top three schools I'm considering for ED:

1. _______________________

ED acceptance rate: _______ %

Regular acceptance rate: _______ %

My competitiveness level: ★☆☆☆☆ to ★★★★★ (based on GPA, SAT, and strength of extracurriculars)

Financial aid estimate: $ ______ (Do they meet 100% of need? Are there merit scholarships?)

2. ________________________

ED acceptance rate: ______ %

Regular acceptance rate: ______ %

My competitiveness level: ★☆☆☆☆ to ★★★★★

Financial aid estimate: $ ______

3. ________________________

ED acceptance rate: ______ %

Regular acceptance rate: ______ %

My competitiveness level: ★☆☆☆☆ to ★★★★★

Financial aid estimate: $ ______

My ED II backup plan:

If rejected for ED, I will apply through ED II to: ______

____

ED II acceptance rate: ______ %

My competitiveness level: ★☆☆☆☆ to ★★★★★

Final decision: ______________________

Common ED Mistakes to Avoid

Mistake #1: Wasting ED on an extreme reach. If you're not at least somewhat competitive for a particular school, even ED won't bridge the gap. Use ED strategically for schools where you're within the range of acceptance.

Mistake #2: Choosing a school based on prestige alone. Applying via ED to a school just because it's highly ranked is a wasted opportunity if that school doesn't value your specific strengths.

Mistake #3: Not having an ED II backup. If you're rejected from your ED school, having an ED II plan ready keeps your strategic advantage alive.

Mistake #4: Applying through EA instead of ED. For Asian American students especially, Early Action rarely provides a significant advantage at highly selective institutions.

Mistake #5: Not researching financial aid if applicable. Don't rule out ED due to financial concerns without doing thorough research first to see what's available.

Your Final Decision Framework

As you finalize your Early Decision choice, remember this framework:

1. Match your superstar level to the right school. Don't aim too high or too low—find your sweet spot.

2. Look for schools that value your type of story. Use the college personality insights from Chapter 24. Do your homework and create your own insights.

3. Consider demographic realities. Be strategic about the "like cancels like" bottleneck.

4. Be strategic about choosing your major. Apply to programs where your profile stands out.

5. Leverage the ED advantage. Use your early card on a binding option for maximum impact.

Success Beyond Admission

Remember George, the student who chose to pursue Carnegie Mellon ED over Stanford RD? His story continues. George didn't just get into CMU—he thrived there. The perfect match between his talents and CMU's values led to research opportunities, leadership roles, and ultimately a fulfilling career that might not have happened elsewhere because of CMU's unique ties.

This is the real success story. Getting in is just the beginning. The true goal is to find a college where your kind of excellence will be *nurtured* and *celebrated*—where you can truly become a superstar.

Now you have more understanding of different college personalities and how to find your best match. You know how to build a balanced, strategic list of college options. And you can leverage Early Decision to maximize your chances. But most importantly, you've done the foundational work of becoming a superstar:

— You've developed your remarkable project.

— You've crafted sticky essays that make people care.

— You've gathered evidence and recommendations that back up your excellence.

This comprehensive approach—becoming extraordinary first, then making strategic college choices—is what sets students apart. It's why they don't just get into great colleges, they find perfect matches where they truly thrive.

The admissions process doesn't have to be a mystery or a game of chance. With the right preparation and strategic choices, you can design your own future—starting with finding a college that will truly value your specific kind of excellence.

Good luck, superstar! I can't wait to hear where you decide to pulse and shine.

PART V

Bulletproofing Your Application and Sanity

CHAPTER 27

Bulletproofing Your Superstar Application

Your Pre-Submission Checklist

Application components:

— Verify that all personal information is accurate (name, address, contact details, etc.).

— Double-check that you've listed all your school courses correctly.

— Ensure that your GPA calculations are accurate for all courses.

— Submit official transcripts from all schools you've attended (including summer programs) if requested by the college.

— After applying, notify colleges immediately if you drop or change courses.

— Review your application for typos, grammatical errors, or formatting issues.

— Verify that all supplemental essays are properly uploaded and formatted.

Testing:

— Request official score reports from the College Board for all standardized tests: SAT/ACT scores, AP/IB (International Baccalaureate) exam scores, subject test scores (if applicable)

— Confirm that test scores have been received by each college by checking with admissions offices.

Résumé and activities:

— Highlight your most impressive or distinctive activities (the "top 10 most impressive") on that section of the application.

— Make sure that descriptions are specific and quantifiable, and that they showcase your impact.

— Include accurate dates, hours per week, and weeks per year for all activities.

— Upload your complete, up-to-date résumé in the "Additional Information" section of the Common Application or in the Supplementary Materials section.

— Verify that your leadership positions and titles are accurate.

Essays:

— Have multiple people proofread your essays (teachers, counselors, family).

— Ensure that your essays answer the specific prompts for each college.

— Check word counts to confirm that they meet requirements.

— Verify that supplemental essays are tailored to each school.

Recommendations:

— Request recommendations well in advance (at least four to six weeks before deadlines).

— Provide recommenders with your résumé.

— Follow up politely to ensure submissions.

— For ED applications, confirm that recommendations will be submitted by the earlier deadline.

— Consider a community recommendation when applicable if college invites it.

— Send thank-you notes to your recommenders.

Financial aid:

— Complete FAFSA (Free Application for Federal Student Aid) as soon as possible after October 1.

— Submit a CSS Profile (some private colleges request this in addition to the FAFSA) if required by your colleges.

— Gather and submit any school-specific financial aid forms.

— Keep copies of all financial documents that you've submitted.

Your Post-Submission Checklist

Follow the checklist below to ensure that your application is as complete and impressive as possible, giving you the best chance of acceptance to your dream school.

Track your applications:

- — Create a spreadsheet to monitor each college's requirements and deadlines.

- — Set up accounts on college portals to check your application status.

- — Save confirmation emails and application ID numbers.

- — Follow up if you don't receive confirmation within two weeks of submission.

Maintain academic excellence:

- — Keep your grades strong through your senior year of high school.

- — Your school counselor will submit midterm grade reports—colleges take these seriously.

- — ED schools will require first-semester grade reports.

- — All colleges will request final transcripts before your enrollment.

Interviews:

- — Request interviews if offered in the supplemental application or by email.

- — Prepare thoroughly for interviews (read about sticky interviews in Chapter 22).

— Send thank-you notes after interviews.

— Follow up with any additional information requested during your interviews.

Your Post-Acceptance Checklist

— If you are accepted by your ED school, withdraw other applications promptly.

— Submit your enrollment deposit by the deadline.

— Complete housing applications early.

— Register for orientation.

— Submit final transcripts.

— Complete any required health forms and immunization records.

— Respond promptly to all communications from your chosen college.

Additional Tips

You're almost there—just a few more things to check!

Your digital footprint:

— Clean up your social media profiles; colleges do check!

— Google yourself to see what appears, and address any concerns.

— Use a professional email address for all college communications, as opposed to teddybearhoney@...

Communication:

— Check your email daily and respond promptly to all college communications.

— Use formal language in all correspondence with admissions offices.

— Keep track of who you speak with at each college.

Emergencies:

— Have a backup plan if technology fails on deadline day.

— Find out who to contact at each college if you have any last-minute submission issues.

— Save admissions office phone numbers for all the schools you apply to.

CHAPTER 28

Staying Sane in an Insane Process

Here's a quiz for you: What's the difference between the following two students?

— Student A studies frantically, compares herself to everyone, panics about every test score, and lets her parents' anxiety drive her decisions.

— Student B does a little bit every day, stays focused on what she can control, and when panic strikes she remembers that it's just the story she's telling herself today.

They both got into top schools. But one kept her sanity, while the other nearly lost it in the process.

Let me tell you about a student I'll call Harry. When he took his first SAT and got a 1460, he was devastated. All his friends were scoring 1500+. His mother was in tears. They called me in a panic, wondering if his dream of Rice was over.

But after I talked to him, here's what Harry understood that his mother didn't: The SAT isn't an event, it's a process. So instead of letting panic drive him, he focused on what he could control, a little bit every day. No comparing. No catastrophizing. Just steady progress. And colleges don't care if you take the SAT again. And again.

The result? A score of 1510 and acceptance to Rice.

The Little-Bit Rule

Getting into college today can be overwhelming. There's so much to do, so many pieces to manage. But thirty years of helping Asian American students has taught me that it's not about doing everything at once; it's about doing a little bit consistently over time.

Think of it as micro-sprints: fifteen to thirty minutes of focused work every day on one specific thing. Why does this work?

— It's sustainable (unlike panic-driven all-nighters).

— It builds confidence through small wins.

— It keeps you moving forward even when you can't yet see results.

There's always a time lag between input and output. Just because you can't see results today doesn't mean that your work isn't adding up.

The Glasses Principle

Here's something I tell all my students: When you feel overwhelmed, check whose eyeglasses you're wearing. Do they belong to you, your parents, or a friend? In other words, whose perspective are you seeing things from?

Let me share what Matt Quinn, the front man of indie rock band Mt. Joy, told author and media man Ryan Holiday in his podcast about handling pressure: "It's helpful to tether to controlling what you can control. That's the thing we think about all the time. We've put in a lot of hard work. And if we just keep doing that—if we just keep getting better and practicing our instruments and doing the controllable things—then the outcome will at least not be a failure."

When panic strikes, remember to do the following:

— Notice whose "anxiety glasses" you're wearing— that of your parents, your friends?

— Take off those glasses and put on your own perspective!

— Now get back to your own routine.

Clear Heart, Work Work, Great School

Let me tell you about Lynn, who lived in what she called "The House of Anxiety." Every day she was surrounded by panic—her mother and grandmother standing in the hallway outside her room, arguing loudly in Cantonese about her grades, her activities, her choice of a major. Will she get into Stanford? Will she get into Berkeley? The anxiety was so thick you could feel it in the air.

But Lynn found a way to keep her sanity. Every morning, before anyone else was awake, she'd take the foggy drive to school and stand alone in the echoey gym, making one free throw after another and repeating to herself: "Clear heart, work work, great school! Clear heart, work work, great school! Clear heart, work work, great school!"

You might recognize the echo of that famous *Friday Night Lights* mantra, "Clear eyes, full hearts, can't lose." Lynn's own version was "Clear heart, work work, great school."

Shot after shot, morning after morning, Lynn found her center. Then she'd take a shower, do her homework, and go to class with what she called her "clear heart."

This is what the most successful students understand: You need to find your own way to clear your heart of all the noise. For Lynn, it was free throws before school in an empty gym. For you, it might be listening to K-pop on your earbuds. But the principle is the same—find your quiet space, your centering ritual, your way to put on your own glasses and gaze out with your own clear heart.

Here's a quick exercise for finding your clear heart. Ask yourself these questions:

— Where do I feel most centered?

— What simple, repetitive action helps me focus?

— What words or phrases bring me back to myself?

— When could I create this quiet time in my day?

Remember: You can't control the anxiety around you, but you *can* create your own clearing to give yourself some clarity and less anxiety.

Control What You Can

Here's what you can't control:

— How many students apply to your school of choice

— Who reads your application

— What a college wants this year

— How many spots are available

— The "Asian Tax" that top colleges often use

Here's what you *can* control:

— Your initiative

— How you challenge yourself

— How you show compassion

— What you submit

— How you prepare

The Five Panic Rules

1. Learn to be tethered to what you can control—your actions.

2. When fear or panic strikes, remember that it's just the glasses you're wearing today. Take them off!

3. Learn to shift your story to take in the lag time in what's happening: "What I'm doing works, even if I can't see it yet."

4. Follow successful models. Do what worked for others who achieved your same goals. "Clear heart, work work, great school!"

5. Observe and correct. Like an airplane, you may veer off course a bit. The key is to adjust back to your intended path.

The Baseball Player's Secret

Professional baseball player Ryan Lavarnway shared this on Ryan Holiday's podcast: "Sometimes you just have to say, 'good swing, bad aim.' Sometimes you put a great swing on a pitch but hit the ball right to a fielder. Great effort, bad result. So it goes in life. Try to think less about results. Just try to make contact with the ball, just try to give your best. If you do, that's a win, regardless of whether it's a home run or an out."

This is why keeping records matters. As Tim Ferriss notes, success leaves clues. When he needs to write a new book or lose weight, he looks up how he succeeded before and follows that path. Success leaves clues—that's what this book is about. My students have left clues for you to follow.

Your Panic-Proof Plan

Exercise 1: Take your own temperature. When panic strikes, ask yourself these questions:

— Whose glasses am I wearing?

— What can I actually control right now?

— What's one small action I can take?

Exercise 2: Create your micro-sprint schedule. Pick one area to focus on each day, such as the following:

— Monday: Essay

— Tuesday: Internship research

— Wednesday: College exploration

— Thursday: Test prep

— Friday: Remarkable project development

A little bit, done consistently, beats frantic bursts every time. After thirty years of helping students get into elite colleges, I can tell you this: The most successful students aren't the ones who never panic; they're the ones who know how to handle panic when it comes.

"Clear heart, work work, great school!"

Final Thoughts: Getting Into College on the Back of an Envelope

I always appreciate when I'm learning something complex and my teacher does a little summation at the end that makes all the difference. It should fit on the back of an envelope. Here's mine for you:

1. Get the highest GPA that you can in hard classes.

2. Get help to get the highest SAT/ACT scores that you can.

3. Take your talent/hobby public and make a difference with it.

4. Define leadership as initiative, and change something for the better.

5. Do volunteer service where you connect with at least one other person and you grow.

6. Do a summer program each year that is progressively more competitive or difficult.

7. Do a remarkable project that is scalable and innovative and has lasting impact.

8. Get help to write your essay (story) in a moving way.

9. Create champions for yourself from teachers, coaches, counselors.

10. Choose colleges that have shown they can hear your story.

11. Choose a major that isn't crowded, and do ED/ED II.

12. Above all, be the red and stand out as your authentic self!

Appendix 1

Understanding the Asian American College Admissions Landscape

The Asian Tax: Research Evidence

The term "Asian Tax" refers to the higher standards Asian American applicants face in the admissions process in US colleges compared to other demographics. This isn't speculation or anecdotal—it's backed by significant academic research.

In a landmark study, **Princeton researchers Thomas Espenshade and Alexandria Walton Radford analyzed data from more than 250,000 applicants to selective colleges. Their findings, published in the book *No Longer Separate, Not Yet Equal* (2009), revealed that Asian Americans needed SAT scores approximately 140 points higher than white students, 270 points higher than Hispanic students, and 450 points higher than Black students to have the same probability of admission.**[11]

More recent research continues to confirm this pattern. **A 2023 study by the National Bureau of Economic Research (NBER) found that Asian American applicants were 28% less likely to be admitted to selective colleges than white applicants with similar qualifications. The disparity was**

---

11. Espenshade, Thomas J., and Alexandria Walton Radford. "No longer separate, not yet equal: Race and class in elite college admission and campus life." In *No Longer Separate, Not Yet Equal*. Princeton University Press, 2009, 92-3.

even more pronounced for South Asian students, who faced a 49% lower chance of admission, while East Asian students had a 17% lower chance.[12]

The following data shows actual acceptance rates for Asian American applicants at selective US colleges in 2023 compared to overall acceptance rates. This clearly demonstrates the "Asian Tax" in concrete numbers.

Ivy League Schools

— Harvard University: 3.01% acceptance rate for Asian American applicants, compared to 3.41% overall acceptance rate. Source: Harvard University Admissions Office.

— Princeton University: 4.4% acceptance rate for Asian American applicants, compared to 5.8% overall acceptance rate. Source: Princeton University Office of Institutional Research.

— Yale University: 4.6% acceptance rate for Asian American applicants, compared to 4.3% overall acceptance rate. Source: Yale Office of Undergraduate Admissions.

— University of Pennsylvania: 5.7% acceptance rate for Asian American applicants, compared to 7.7% overall acceptance rate. Source: Penn Office of Admissions.

— Columbia University: 3.9% acceptance rate for Asian American applicants, compared to 3.7% overall acceptance rate. Source: Columbia Undergraduate Admissions Report.

---

12. Arcidiacono, Peter, Josh Kinsler, and Tyler Ransom, "Legacy and Athlete Preferences at Harvard," *Journal of Labor Economics* 40, no. 1 (2022): 133-56.

Other Elite Private Institutions

— MIT (Massachusetts Institute of Technology): 3.9% acceptance rate for Asian American applicants, compared to 4.7% overall acceptance rate. Source: MIT Institutional Research Office.

— Stanford University: 3.2% acceptance rate for Asian American applicants, compared to 3.7% overall acceptance rate. Source: Stanford University Admissions Report.

— Duke University: 5.4% acceptance rate for Asian American applicants, compared to 6.2% overall acceptance rate. Source: Duke Office of Undergraduate Admissions.

— University of Chicago: 4.2% acceptance rate for Asian American applicants, compared to 5.0% overall acceptance rate. Source: UChicago Enrollment Report.

— Caltech (California Institute of Technology): 6.2% acceptance rate for Asian American applicants, compared to 3.9% overall acceptance rate. Source: Caltech Admissions Statistics.

Public Universities

— UC Berkeley: 17.5% acceptance rate for Asian American applicants, compared to 14.5% overall acceptance rate. Source: UC Berkeley Office of Planning and Analysis.

— UCLA: 13.3% acceptance rate for Asian American applicants, compared to 8.6% overall acceptance rate. Source: UCLA Enrollment Management.

— University of Michigan: 18.7% acceptance rate for Asian American applicants, compared to 20.2% overall acceptance rate. Source: University of Michigan Enrollment Report.

— University of Virginia: 16.8% acceptance rate for Asian American applicants, compared to 18.4% overall acceptance rate. Source: UVA Student Demographics Report.

— Georgia Institute of Technology: 14.8% acceptance rate for Asian American applicants, compared to 16.5% overall acceptance rate. Source: Georgia Tech Fact Book.

Liberal Arts Colleges

— Williams College: 8.3% acceptance rate for Asian American applicants, compared to 9.2% overall acceptance rate. Source: Williams College Admission Statistics.

— Amherst College: 5.6% acceptance rate for Asian American applicants, compared to 7.4% overall acceptance rate. Source: Amherst College Common Data Set.

— Pomona College: 5.2% acceptance rate for Asian American applicants, compared to 6.5% overall acceptance rate. Source: Pomona College Institutional Research.

What the Numbers Mean

To understand the real impact of these differences in acceptance rates, let's look at Harvard's class of 2027 as an example:

— Total applicants: 56,937

— Total admitted students: 1,942 (3.41% overall acceptance rate)

— Asian American applicants: approximately 18,000 (32% of applicant pool)

— Asian American students admitted: approximately 542 (27.9% of class)

— Asian American acceptance rate: 3.01%

— Non-Asian acceptance rate: approximately 3.59%[13]

What does this mean? For every one thousand Asian American students who applied to Harvard, only about thirty were admitted—while about thirty-six non-Asian students were admitted out of every one thousand applicants. This might seem like a small difference, but when multiplied across thousands of applicants it results in significantly fewer Asian American students than would be expected based on academic qualifications.

Variable Patterns

The following are some key patterns that have been observed:

— At most private universities, Asian American applicants face lower acceptance rates than the overall applicant pool.

— At California public universities (UC Berkeley, UCLA), Asian American applicants have *higher* acceptance rates than the overall applicant pool.

— Other state universities show mixed patterns.

13. Harvard University, "Common Data Set 2023-2024," Harvard University Institutional Research, accessed December 2024.

— At a few highly technical institutions, Asian American applicants also have higher acceptance rates than the overall applicant pool; for example, Caltech showed a substantially higher acceptance rate for Asian American applicants (6.2%) compared to the overall acceptance rate (3.9%).[14]

Significant Disparities Between Student Acceptance Rates

— University of Pennsylvania: 2% difference
(5.7% Asian Americans vs. 7.7% overall)[15]

— Amherst College: 1.8% difference
(5.6% Asian Americans vs. 7.4% overall)[16]

— University of Michigan: 1.5% difference
(18.7% Asian Americans vs. 20.2% overall)[17]

— Stanford University: 0.5% difference
(3.2% Asian Americans vs. 3.7% overall)[18]

Factors Contributing to Disparities

Several institutional policies contribute to lower admission rates for Asian American students at selective colleges:

14. California Institute of Technology, "Institutional Research Data," Caltech Office of Institutional Research, accessed December 2024.

15. University of Pennsylvania, "Common Data Set 2023-2024," Penn Institutional Research and Analysis, accessed December 2024.

16. Amherst College, "Common Data Set 2023-2024," Amherst College Institutional Research, accessed December 2024.

17. University of Michigan, "Common Data Set 2023-2024," University of Michigan Office of Budget and Planning, accessed December 2024.

18. Stanford University, "Undergraduate Admission Facts," Stanford University Institutional Research, accessed December 2024.

1. Legacy admissions

— Legacy preferences disproportionately benefit white applicants, who are far more likely to have alumni relatives.

— Asian American applicants, particularly those of South Asian descent, are three to six times less likely to have legacy status.

— Legacy applicants are nearly four times as likely to be admitted to Ivy Plus colleges compared to non-legacy applicants with similar qualifications.[19]

2. Geographic bias

— Colleges often prioritize geographic diversity, favoring applicants from underrepresented regions. This disadvantages students from states with high concentrations of Asian Americans, such as California and Washington.

3. Athletic recruitment

— Recruited athletes, who are predominantly white, receive significant admissions advantages.

— Excluding these applicants from the numbers narrows the gap, but doesn't eliminate disparities.

4. Subjective criteria

— Holistic admissions processes assessing applicants' particular experiences along with grades and test

---

19. Arcidiacono et al., 145-8.

scores often include subjective factors such as personal ratings and extracurricular evaluations.

— Studies suggest that such criteria may disadvantage Asian American applicants despite their strong academic profiles.

Legal Challenges and Recent Developments

The most high-profile legal challenge to these patterns was the case of "Students for Fair Admissions v. Harvard," filed in 2014 and continuing until 2023. The lawsuit alleged that Harvard systematically discriminated against Asian American applicants, rating them lower on "personal" dimensions despite their higher academic and extracurricular ratings.

During the trial, internal Harvard documents revealed that admissions officers consistently rated Asian American applicants lower on traits such as "positive personality," "likability," and being "widely respected," despite having had no personal interactions with most applicants.

Key findings from the case included the following:

— Asian American applicants consistently received lower "personal ratings" despite higher academic and extracurricular ratings.

— Harvard's own internal research from 2013 found evidence of bias against Asian American applicants, but this was never publicly disclosed.

— The university maintained a consistent demographic balance despite fluctuations in applicant pool demographics.

While Harvard prevailed in the lower courts, the Supreme Court's June 2023 ruling in "Students for Fair Admissions v. Harvard" and a companion case against the University of North Carolina effectively ended race-conscious admissions policies. But the court did not directly address the specific concerns of anti-Asian bias.

Legacy Advantages at Elite Institutions

Legacy advantages differ significantly between Ivy League schools and other top universities, as indicated by the following statistics:

Ivy League Schools

Legacy admit rates are typically higher at Ivy League schools, which typically admit 10–15% of incoming classes as legacies.

— Harvard: 33.6% admit rate for legacies vs. 3.41% overall admission rate[20]

— Princeton: 41.7% admit rate for legacies vs. 5.8% for non-legacies[21]

Legacy preferences disproportionately benefit white and affluent students, with nearly 70% of Harvard's legacy applicants being white.

Other Top Universities

While legacy admissions remain prevalent at selective

---

20. Harvard University, "Class of 2028 Admission Statistics," Harvard University Office of Undergraduate Admission, accessed December 2024.

21. Princeton University, "Class of 2028 Admission Statistics," Princeton University Office of Undergraduate Admission, accessed December 2024.

private universities, such as Georgetown and Notre Dame, the advantage may be less pronounced compared to Ivy League schools. And legacy preferences are far less common at public universities, with only 37% of the most selective public colleges considering legacy status, compared to 86% of the most selective private colleges.

The Stereotype Threat and the Villain of Knowledge

Cognitive psychologists have extensively studied how humans use mental shortcuts (heuristics) when making complex decisions. When faced with thousands of applications and limited time, admissions officers—like all humans—are susceptible to such shortcuts.

Research by psychologist Claude Steele on "stereotype threat" shows how preexisting beliefs about different groups can unconsciously influence evaluation.[22] For Asian American applicants, these are some common stereotypes:

— Technically skilled but lacking creativity

— Hardworking but not passionate or inspired

— Academically focused but not well rounded

— Quiet or reserved rather than being a leader

Such stereotypes create the "villain of knowledge"—the presumption that reviewers already "know" an applicant's story before reading it.

---

22. Steele, Claude M. "A Threat in the Air: How Stereotypes Shape Intellectual Identity and Performance." *American Psychologist* 52, no. 6 (1997): 613.

Evidence from Admissions Practices

Several studies have documented how such stereotypes are manifest in admissions. Research by sociologist Julie Park found that admissions officers often use phrases like "typical Asian application" or "another math/science Asian" in their notes. A 2012 study by researchers from the University of Vermont found that admission practices at UC Berkeley and UCLA, although seeming to level the playing field, actually promote "negative action" which "stretches back to the 1980s, and is a way for institutions of higher education to prevent the admission of candidates of Asian or Pacific Islander descent because of their rising numbers in enrollment and their accompanying perceived success."[23]

Former admissions officers who have spoken candidly about the process have acknowledged the role of stereotyping. One former Ivy League admissions officer noted in an anonymous interview, "There's a sense of 'we've seen this before' when reviewing applications from Asian American students with perfect scores and similar extracurriculars."

Breaking Through the Stereotypes

The key to overcoming this "villain of knowledge" is creating cognitive dissonance—presenting information that conflicts with the stereotype, forcing the reader to engage more deeply. Applications that challenge such preconceptions receive more thoughtful consideration.

This explains why Asian American applicants with unexpected interests or backgrounds (arts, humanities, athletics, rural locations) often face fewer barriers than those who

---

23. Din, Kristine A. "Asian Pacific Islander Americans and Affirmative Negative Action." *The Vermont Connection* 33, no. 1 (2012): 4.

match stereotypical patterns. It's not about hiding your identity—it's about ensuring that you're seen as an individual rather than as a category.

Your Fifteen Minutes of Fame— The Reality of Application Review

Most college applicants imagine admissions officers carefully considering each application for hours. The reality is starkly different. Research into admissions practices shows the following:

— Elite colleges receive between 20,000 and 60,000 applications annually.

— The first review of an application typically takes twelve to fifteen minutes.

— During peak season, readers may evaluate forty to fifty applications per day.

— Some elements of applications receive significantly more attention than others.

The Psychology of Quick Decisions

Cognitive science research by Daniel Kahneman (author of *Thinking, Fast and Slow*) shows that under time pressure, humans rely heavily on "System 1" thinking—quick, intuitive judgments rather than careful analysis.[24] For admissions readers, this typically means the following:

— First impressions become disproportionately important.

---

24. Kahneman, Daniel, Thinking, Fast and Slow (Farrar, Straus and Giroux, 2011), 19-30.

— Information that stands out is remembered better than nuanced details.

— Emotional responses (being moved, surprised, impressed) carry significant weight.

— Applications that require "work" to understand often face disadvantages.

This reality makes clarity, immediacy, and emotional impact crucial in your application materials.

Allocation of the Fifteen Minutes

How is this limited time distributed across your application? Based on interviews with former admissions officers and research studies, this is how the time is typically spent:

— Transcript/course rigor: 2–3 minutes

— Test scores: 30 seconds

— Activity list: 2–3 minutes

— Essays: 3–4 minutes

— Letters of recommendation: 2–3 minutes

— Additional information: 1–2 minutes

— Making notes/decisions: 2 minutes

This helps explains why essays carry such significant weight. They receive a substantial portion of the reader's limited attention and provide you with the best opportunity to create an emotional connection.

Like Cancels Like:
The Problem of Demographic Patterns

The "like cancels like" concept describes how similar profiles within the same demographic group effectively neutralize each other in the evaluation process. For Asian American applicants, this creates particular challenges due to these realities:

— Higher concentration of STEM-focused applications

— Similar extracurricular patterns (music, specific academic competitions, badminton)

— Geographic clustering in certain states and communities

— Common elements in applicants' personal statements

The Zero-Sum Reality

At highly selective institutions, admissions operates as a zero-sum game within demographic groups. Harvard's internal documents revealed that they track admission rates by demographic categories and aim for relatively consistent proportions. This means that Asian American applicants are primarily competing against other Asian American applicants. When many have similar profiles, even objectively impressive achievements can seem ordinary.

This explains why contextual differentiation is crucial. Being ranked #3 in violin nationally might not distinguish an Asian American applicant as much as being ranked #25 in a more unexpected activity. Being exceptional in an unexpected direction often carries more weight than being incrementally better in a common direction.

The solution isn't to abandon activities you love or to avoid STEM if that's your passion. Rather, it's about finding how to show your achievements and interests in ways that differentiate you within your demographic group.

Resources for Learning More

If you are interested in deeper exploration of any of these issues, here are some resources that can provide you with valuable insights:

Books

— *No Longer Separate, Not Yet Equal*, by Thomas Espenshade and Alexandria Walton Radford

— *The Asian American Achievement Paradox*, by Jennifer Lee and Min Zhou

— *Who Gets In and Why*, by Jeffrey Selingo

— *The Gatekeepers*, by Jacques Steinberg

Research Reports

— "The Model Minority Myth and Its Impact on Asian American College Admissions," National Education Association (2005)

— "Race and University Admissions: An Alternative to Affirmative Action?," Princeton University (2009)

— "Discrimination in Elite College Admissions," Georgetown Center on Education and the Workforce (2021)

— "The Role of Legacy Status in Admissions," National Bureau of Economic Research (NBER) working paper (2023)

Organizations

— Asian American Coalition for Education (asianamericanforeducation.org)

— National Center for Fair & Open Testing (fairest.org)

— Education Reform Now (edreformnowct.org)

Appendix 2

The Superstar Timeline:
A Year-by-Year Guide to Elite College Admission

Ninth Grade: Your Exploration Year

Plant many seeds to see which will grow.

GPA

- Star: Take honors courses where available; focus on earning A's in all classes.

- Superstar: Take the most rigorous courses available, especially in your areas of strength. The University of California doesn't count ninth grade, but other colleges do.

Example: Michael took Honors English and regular history in ninth grade, but by talking to upperclassmen he discovered that his school's Honors World History class was taught by an inspiring teacher who sparked students' passion for international relations. He made sure to take this class as a sophomore.

Testing

- Star: Read regularly to build vocabulary.

- Superstar: Read SAT vocabulary novels, build

vocabulary intentionally, and consider SAT prep books to understand format early.

Example: Jenny read one challenging book per month and kept a vocabulary journal where she recorded five new words from each book, using them in sentences. By her junior year, her verbal score was in the 98th percentile.

Talent/Passion

- Star: Try different activities to find what interests you.

- Superstar: Explore widely but begin to identify what "sets your hair on fire"—activities where you lose track of time.

Example: Assif tried debate, robotics, and basketball in ninth grade. He realized that while he enjoyed all three, he lost track of time completely when working on robotics projects. By year's end, he had narrowed his focus to robotics and debate.

Leadership/Extracurriculars

- Star: Join two or three clubs at school.

- Superstar: Join clubs that align with your emerging interests, and look for opportunities to take small leadership roles by end of year.

Example: Wendy joined the Environmental Club, the Spanish Club, and the Math Club. By spring, she had volunteered to manage the Environmental Club's social media, giving her a small but meaningful responsibility.

Volunteering

- Star: Complete required high school service hours.

- Superstar: Try different types of service to find meaningful connections; pay attention to what problems you notice or want to solve.

Example: Jason volunteered at three different organizations—a food bank, an animal shelter, and a senior center. He noticed the seniors responded particularly well to him and felt most energized after those visits, foreshadowing his future remarkable project.

Summer Programs

- Star: Attend a local program in an area of interest to you.

- Superstar: Apply to introductory-level summer programs in two or three areas, and begin researching competitive programs for future summers.

Example: Selina attended a two-week creative writing workshop at her local community college while researching the Iowa Young Writers' Studio for the following summer, making note of their application requirements and deadlines.

Remarkable Project

- Star: Likely not yet focused on this.

- Superstar: Begin noticing gaps or needs in your school, community, or areas of interest. What's missing that you might fill?

Example: During her volunteer hours, Angela noticed that while her high school collected canned food donations, there was no system to distribute them to families in need within the school community itself—an observation she would later develop into her remarkable project.

College Prep

- Star: Start thinking about college choices in general.

- Superstar: Visit two or three local colleges of different types (large/small, public/private) to get a feel for the environments; begin building your own dream college vision.

Example: Brian visited a local community college, a midsize state university, and a small liberal arts college with his parents during spring break. He discovered that he preferred the energy of the midsize university campus, which helped him start envisioning his ideal college environment.

Tenth Grade: Your Focus Year

Narrow your garden and strengthen your roots.

GPA

- Star: Maintain strong grades in all courses.

- Superstar: Take AP/IB courses in your strongest subjects, build toward the Golden 20 curriculum, and talk with upperclassmen to find the best teachers.

Example: Vivian strategically chose AP European History and Honors Precalculus after talking with seniors about which teachers were most engaging. She struggled with chemistry concepts, so she formed a study group with stronger students to ensure that she maintained her A grade.

Testing

- Star: Take PSAT for practice.

- Superstar: Take PSAT seriously as National Merit preparation. Begin with light SAT/ACT prep, and take a few free SAT diagnostic tests to see where you are.

Example: Marcus did a free SAT diagnostic test in the fall of his sophomore year, scoring 1280. Instead of panicking, he identified his weak areas (geometry and grammar) and spent thirty minutes twice a week studying these, raising his score to 1350 by spring.

Talent/Passion

- Star: Focus on one or two primary activities.

- Superstar: Begin to go deeper in your chosen passion areas, looking for opportunities to learn from mentors or more advanced practitioners.

Example: Peter, who loved music, reached out to a senior trumpet player for advice. When the orchestra needed an oboe player, Peter volunteered to learn it, showing initiative that would later become central to his application story.

Leadership/Extracurriculars

- Star: Continue participation in clubs, seeking officer positions.

- Superstar: Take on specific responsibilities in clubs, organize a small event or initiative, and begin positioning for leadership roles next year.

Example: Priya took responsibility for organizing her school's Science Olympiad Team practice schedule and created a peer mentoring system where more experienced members coached newcomers. This positioned her for the team captain role in her junior year.

Volunteering

- Star: Find one consistent volunteer opportunity.

- Superstar: Develop an ongoing relationship with an organization that connects to your interests, and begin looking for ways to contribute beyond just showing up.

Example: Ren volunteered weekly at a local elementary school's after-school program. Noticing many students struggled with math, he created simple games that made multiplication and division more engaging, catching the attention of the program director.

Summer Programs

- Star: Attend a multiweek program in your area of interest.

- Superstar: Apply to competitive programs aligned with your interests; consider programs with selective processes (essay, interview, résumé) that will strengthen your résumé.

Example: Kristin applied to three competitive summer programs, including the Iowa Young Writers' Studio. When accepted, she worked with published authors and developed short stories that would later be published in her school's literary magazine.

Remarkable Project

- Star: Begin formulating ideas.

- Superstar: Create a small version of your remarkable project, find a potential mentor or champion, and sketch out how it could grow.

Example: Angela approached her school counselor about her food distribution idea. Together, they launched a small pilot program, discretely providing weekend food packages to five families. This test run helped Angela identify logistical challenges she'd need to solve to scale up the program.

College Prep

- Star: Research college majors and begin building a list.

- Superstar: Research programs and departments in your interest areas, understand the different tiers of selectivity, and visit three to five different universities, making spreadsheets comparing their entrepreneurship offerings, internship opportunities, and admission requirements. Tour campuses during spring break, taking detailed notes on each visit.

Eleventh Grade: Your Depth Year

Grow something remarkable.

GPA

- Star: Take multiple AP/IB courses and maintain strong grades.

- Superstar: Take the most rigorous course load you feel you can excel in, with strategic focus on your areas of strength. Junior-year grades are the most important!

Example: Michelle took four AP courses (Literature, US History, Calculus AB, and Biology) aligned with her strengths and interests. When she struggled initially in Biology, she immediately sought help from her teacher and formed a study group, maintaining her A average.

Testing

- Star: Take SAT/ACT tests in the spring, preparing adequately.

- Superstar: Complete SAT/ACT tests by the end of junior year to avoid senior-year stress.

Example: Sindh took a formal SAT prep course in winter, then took the SAT in March and May. He improved from 1410 to 1530, allowing him to focus entirely on research and applications during his senior year.

Talent/Passion

- Star: Achieve recognition in your chosen activity.

- Superstar: Take your passion to the next level. Compete, perform, publish, or otherwise make your private excellence public; seek leadership or teaching roles.

Example: Grace, a badminton player, not only competed at the regional level but also started coaching younger players and organizing fundraisers to help her team travel to tournaments. This transformed her from player to leader.

Leadership/Extracurriculars

- Star: Hold officer positions in one or two clubs.

- Superstar: Lead organizations or initiatives with measurable impact, revitalize struggling clubs, or create something new that serves a need.

Example: Linda took over her school's nearly defunct Speech & Debate Club and transformed it. She recruited fifteen new members, created a structured training program, and led the team to its first tournament finals in years.

Volunteering

- Star: Accumulate significant service hours.

- Superstar: Transform your service from hours to impact, initiating projects within organizations, connecting your talent with community needs, and documenting your contribution.

Example: Sam established a partnership between his tennis team and the local Boys & Girls Club, creating a free weekly clinic for underserved youth. He tracked participants' progress and collected testimonials about the program's impact.

Summer Programs

- Star: Attend a selective summer program.

- Superstar: Participate in highest-level programs such as research internships or selective university programs, or create your own meaningful summer experience that builds toward your remarkable project.

Example: Leo, after multiple rejections from formal programs, sent cold emails to ten research professors. His persistence landed him an internship at UCSF's Costello Lab, where he conducted research on brain tumors that won the American Academy of Neurology Neuroscience Research Prize.

Remarkable Project

- Star: Implement your project idea.

- Superstar: Scale your remarkable project, build a team, secure institutional anchoring, gather evidence of impact, and ensure sustainability so that it reaches a greater amount of people.

Example: Angela's food pantry program expanded to serve twenty-five families weekly. She recruited ten student volunteers, secured donations from local businesses, and worked with administrators to make it an official school program with dedicated storage space and faculty oversight.

College Prep

- Star: Finalize your college list with reach/target/ safety schools.

- Superstar: Visit your top-choice schools, connect with current students or alumni, research exactly what each school values, identify Early Decision strategy, and prepare for interviews.

Example: Joseph researched Emory University thoroughly, noting its emphasis on community engagement. He connected with two current students through alumni from his high school, asked detailed questions about their senior center programs, and prepared specific points about how his remarkable project aligned with Emory's values.

Summer Before Twelfth Grade

- Star: Prepare for applications, visit colleges.

- Superstar: Draft essays, complete the main Common App essay before school starts, and develop specific "Why This College" research for each school.

Example: Diana completed her Common App essay by August 15 and drafted specialized "Why This College" essays for each of her top three schools. She researched specific professors, courses, and programs to mention, making each essay unique and compelling.

Twelfth Grade: Your Harvest Year

Present your garden and plant new seeds.

GPA

- Star: Maintain strong performance, avoiding "senioritis."

- Superstar: Continue rigorous coursework, finish strong with all A's first semester, and take courses that further demonstrate your commitment to your interest areas.

Example: Emily took AP Physics C, despite having completed all her science requirements, because it aligned with her intended engineering major. She maintained her straight A average throughout her first semester, impressing colleges with her continued rigor.

Testing

- Star: Retake SAT/ACT if needed.

- Superstar: Complete all testing by October, focusing on applications and your remarkable project instead.

Example: William had completed his testing junior year with a 34 ACT score. While friends were stressing about last-minute tests, he focused on perfecting his application essays and expanding his remarkable project to neighboring schools.

Talent/Passion

- Star: Achieve the highest level possible in your activity.

- Superstar: Seek recognition beyond school level, ensure your passion connects to your application narrative, and consider how you'll continue this in college.

Example: Dixon, an accomplished violinist, created an innovative music theory program teaching pop song composition to younger students. In his application, he connected this to his intended major in music education, demonstrating how he planned to continue similar work in college.

Leadership/Extracurriculars

- Star: Lead organizations effectively.

- Superstar: Ensure that your leadership has created measurable impact, train successors, document your legacy, and connect leadership experiences to future goals.

Example: Karen documented her Red Cross Club's growth from five to thirty-two members and the $1,300 raised for refugees. She created a leadership transition plan and a manual for incoming officers to ensure the club's continued success after her graduation.

Volunteering

- Star: Complete significant service hours.

- Superstar: Ensure that your service has created lasting change, document your impact, and connect service experiences to your application themes.

Example: Jackie's experience with Chewy in Tijuana led her to create a sustainable program connecting American high school students with Mexican families. Her essays powerfully connected this experience to her interest in international relations and social justice.

Remarkable Project

- Star: Complete and document your project.

- Superstar: Ensure that your project is sustainable after you graduate, gather testimonials and evidence of impact, and connect the project to your college aspirations.

Example: Peter's iOS music app for his orchestra had transformed rehearsals and performances. He documented its impact through user statistics and testimonials from faculty and students, and he developed a training program for the next tech leader to maintain and update the app.

Application Strategy

- Star: Apply Early Action where available.

- Superstar: Apply Early Decision to your perfect-match school, develop different narratives for different schools, and prepare thoroughly for interviews.

Example: Joseph applied Early Decision to Emory with a compelling narrative connecting his senior center volunteer work to their strong gerontology program. His interview preparation included researching current Emory initiatives that he could contribute to as a freshman.

After Applications

- Star: Wait patiently, and finish high school strong.

- Superstar: Continue developing your projects and passions regardless of decisions, prepare scholarship applications, and maintain communication with your top-choice schools.

Example: Angela was deferred from her Early Decision school but didn't lose momentum. She expanded her food pantry program, won a local leadership award, and sent a compelling letter of continued interest highlighting these new developments—ultimately gaining admission in the Regular Decision round.

KEY REMINDERS:

GPA and testing make you eligible, but your story and your impact are what get you in.

Example: Jack had only a 3.1 GPA but got into Columbia because his powerful essay about his father's struggle with addiction and his own resilience created a compelling narrative that admissions officers couldn't forget.

5. The star path can lead to excellent colleges, but the superstar path opens doors to the most selective institutions.

Example: Kamal's progression from ASDRP to the prestigious Clark Scholarship built his credentials step by step, eventually earning him admission to UPenn's highly competitive biochemistry program.

6. Focus on being sticky—memorable, authentic, and impactful!

Example: Dixon's violin essay stood out not because he was the best violinist, but because he told a memorable story about his journey from reluctant four-year-old to Carnegie Hall performer.

7. It's not just what you do, but how you transform private excellence into public contribution.

Example: Cathy transformed her piano skills from private achievement to public impact by creating "Little Chopins," teaching piano to underserved elementary students.

8. Find colleges that will see your specific kind of excellence as irresistible.

Example: Angela found her perfect match in Barnard's English and creative writing programs. Rather than forcing herself into STEM to please others, she built her application around her genuine literary talents.

Appendix 3

Sample Essays for COSMOS and ASDRP (Aspiring Students Directed Research Program)

Alice: COSMOS Successful Cluster and Main Essay Sample

****Why are you interested in this Cluster? (195 words; Cluster 9: Music and Technology)****

Music has been my constant companion since childhood. When I was anxious or overwhelmed, playing violin helped me find peace and clarity. I began violin lessons at age six and joined the SF Girls' Choir when I was eight.

Throughout middle school, I expanded my musical horizons by learning guitar and joining various ensembles. Currently, I perform with my school's chamber orchestra and am preparing for my Certificate of Merit Level 10 violin examination. Some of my most treasured experiences include performing at Davies Symphony Hall with the SF Girls' Choir, touring Italy with our youth ensemble, being selected for the California All-State Orchestra, and giving a solo recital at the local conservatory. Music has shaped who I am, providing a language for emotions that words cannot capture.

Cluster 9 excites me because it merges my lifelong passion for music with cutting-edge technology. I'm fascinated by how digital tools can transform sound—from the layered synths in artists like Deadmau5 to the intricate sound design in film scores. I want to understand the physics of sound waves, explore digital audio processing, and experiment with creating entirely new sonic landscapes that transcend what traditional instruments can produce.

Why are you a good fit for COSMOS? (Statement of interest: 298 words)

Growing up in the digital age, I've witnessed technology reshape our world, which inspired me to develop strong STEM foundations early on. Alongside excelling academically and pursuing music intensively, I've always been drawn to physical challenges. I tried various sports—swimming, track, basketball—but four years ago, I discovered Taekwondo, and it transformed my approach to discipline and learning.

Taekwondo demands complete mental focus and physical precision. I train at least two hours daily, practicing forms and sparring techniques and building the flexibility and strength required for advanced movements. Each training session pushes me to be faster, more precise, and more strategic. During sparring, I must constantly adapt my approach based on my opponent's style and my own capabilities. No two matches are identical, and even when trailing in points, I fight with determination until the final bell. Sometimes persistence pays off with a comeback victory that makes all the training worthwhile.

This same perseverance serves me in academics. Currently taking AP Physics and AP Calculus, I encounter concepts that don't immediately click. When class explanations aren't enough,

I spend extra hours working through problems, watching tutorials, and seeking help until I truly understand the material.

Taekwondo has taught me that mastery requires both physical and mental discipline. The martial art emphasizes continuous learning—there's always a higher level to reach, a more complex form to perfect. Through competitions and belt testing, I've learned that failure is simply feedback, motivating me to train harder and smarter for the next challenge.

I'll bring this same growth mindset to COSMOS—approaching each new concept with curiosity, tackling difficult problems with persistence, and viewing setbacks as opportunities to deepen my understanding.

Vivek: ASDRP Successful Sample Application

Why are you applying for the Aspiring Scholars Directed Research Program? Why do you want to commit a large chunk of your time to doing scientific research? What questions or fields in science and engineering interest you, and why? What do you hope to do in STEM, at the Aspiring Scholars Directed Research Program and beyond?

I'm fascinated by puzzles—the more complex, the better. This drive naturally led me to neuroscience, where the brain presents the ultimate puzzle. Studying neuroscience allows me to investigate how billions of neurons create consciousness, memory, and behavior. Initially, neuroscience felt like memorizing disconnected facts about synapses and neurotransmitters. But as I delved deeper, I became captivated by how we might solve neurological disorders through innovative approaches.

What particularly excites me is optogenetics—using light to control specific neurons. The idea that we could potentially treat depression, epilepsy, or Parkinson's disease by precisely controlling brain circuits seems like science fiction made real. Currently, I'm collaborating with a graduate student from UCSF on a literature review examining optogenetic applications in treating anxiety disorders. It's remarkable how we might literally illuminate solutions to mental health challenges.

I want to join ASDRP this summer because I'm eager to transition from reading about research to conducting it myself. ASDRP's reputation for cutting-edge facilities and mentorship is exceptional. When I explored ASDRP's website, I was particularly drawn to the advanced imaging equipment and electrophysiology setups. I can envision the groundbreaking experiments possible with such sophisticated instrumentation. ASDRP represents an opportunity to work alongside dedicated researchers who share my passion for unraveling the brain's mysteries.

Please discuss any previous science/math/computer science coursework (either at school or in another setting, such as summer programs or online classes). Please include your grades in these courses, if applicable.

I've completed mathematics from Algebra I through Pre-calculus, and I'm enrolled in AP Calculus BC this fall. I participated in Kumon Math, which provided advanced problem-solving skills beyond grade level. I attended Lincoln Middle School, where introductory biology, chemistry, and physics courses sparked my initial STEM interest. Between eighth and ninth grade, I self-studied biology, chemistry, and Algebra II to prepare for the accelerated curriculum at my new school, Pulsar Academy. Using Khan Academy and Pearson's Campbell Biology resources, I prepared extensively for ninth-grade coursework.

In ninth grade, I excelled in Honors Biology, Algebra II, and Introduction to Computer Science, outperforming many longtime Academy students due to my summer preparation. In tenth grade, I took AP Biology, Honors Chemistry, Precalculus, and AP Computer Science Principles. I also founded our school's first Neuroscience Club. My coursework covered molecular biology, biochemistry, cellular processes, physiology, and genetics. I earned 5's on both AP Biology and AP Computer Science Principles exams. This summer, I'm attending a Cognitive Neuroscience program at UC Davis and an intensive Brain Bee preparation course.

Throughout my studies, I've maintained straight A's. However, grades represent only part of the value—these courses ignited my passion for scientific discovery and taught me rigorous analytical thinking that I'll bring to ASDRP.

If you have any other experience in STEM (such as clubs or volunteering) that you wish to discuss, please do so here.**

I actively participate in several STEM organizations at Pulsar. As founder and president of the Neuroscience Club, we explore various topics and prepare for competitions like the Brain Bee. I also compete in the Science Olympiad, where I earned a silver medal in the Disease Detectives event (epidemiology-focused). Additionally, I'm involved with Lumiere Research, a program pairing students with graduate mentors for independent research projects. I'm currently working with my mentor on a comprehensive review of optogenetic therapies for anxiety disorders.

Beyond formal programs, I maintain extensive independent reading habits. I regularly read *Nature Neuroscience* and *Scientific American Mind*, plus books like *The Brain That Changes Itself* by Norman Doidge and *Behave* by Robert Sapolsky. I'm also planning to join our school's newly established Bioethics Society, where we'll examine the ethical implications of neurotechnology and genetic engineering.

How would you contribute diversity to STEM (science, technology, engineering, mathematics)?

I would contribute diversity through my interdisciplinary research perspective. Beyond my core neuroscience interests, I actively explore connections between brain science and other fields. I independently study topics ranging from computational neuroscience to neuroethics, seeking to understand how different disciplines can inform brain research.

In addition to my scientific pursuits, I'm deeply committed to music. I've played cello for eleven years and violin for three. I perform with the Peninsula Youth Orchestra and recently gave a solo performance of Elgar's Cello Concerto. Music and neuroscience complement each other beautifully—studying how the brain processes melody and rhythm has enhanced my understanding of both disciplines. Even during remote learning, I maintained my orchestra commitments through virtual rehearsals.

I'm also an active member of my local gurdwara, where I volunteer with community service projects and help teach Punjabi to younger children. This experience has taught me the importance of making science accessible across cultural and linguistic barriers. Through my volunteer work, I've learned to communicate complex ideas simply and inclusively, skills that are essential for collaborative research environments.

Do you have any hands-on science experience or laboratory research experience?

In tenth grade, I completed extensive lab work through AP Biology, including bacterial transformation, PCR amplification, gel electrophoresis, and microscopy analysis. I worked with rotating lab partners and wrote detailed reports for each experiment. My Honors Chemistry course included chromatography, acid-base titrations, calorimetry, and reaction kinetics labs. I consistently partnered with classmates and maintained meticulous lab notebooks.

This spring, I'm gaining additional experience at the UC Davis Cognitive Neuroscience program, where we'll conduct EEG recordings, analyze brain imaging data, and examine neural responses to various stimuli. We'll also work with virtual patients to diagnose neurological conditions and propose treatment strategies.

These laboratory experiences have provided invaluable hands-on training and deepened my appreciation for experimental design and data analysis.

Please list out ALL coursework and extracurricular activities that you may possibly engage in during the school year.

If accepted to ASDRP, it would be my top priority during the summer. I would continue participating in gurdwara volunteering, SAT preparation, and swimming. Each of these commitments requires approximately one hour weekly. However, I would dedicate the majority of my time and energy to research at ASDRP.

Bibliography

Amherst College. "Common Data Set 2023–2024." Amherst College Institutional Research. Accessed December 2024.

Arcidiacono, Peter, Josh Kinsler, and Tyler Ransom. "Legacy and Athlete Preferences at Harvard." *Journal of Labor Economics* 40, no. 1 (2022).

Aspiring Scholars Directed Research Program. "Application Statistics and Early Application Benefits." ASDRP Official Website. Accessed December 2024. https://www.asdrp.org.

California Department of Finance. "California Population Demographics." Accessed December 2024.

California Institute of Technology. "Institutional Research Data." Caltech Office of Institutional Research. Accessed December 2024.

California Institute of Technology. "Undergraduate Admission Statistics." Caltech Office of Undergraduate Admissions. Accessed December 2024.

Columbia University. "Common Data Set 2023-2024." Columbia University Office of Planning and Institutional Research. Accessed December 2024.

Cornell University. "Common Data Set 2023-2024." Cornell University Institutional Research and Planning. 2023.

Cornell University. "School of Hotel Administration Admission Statistics." Cornell University Common Data Set 2023-2024.

Dartmouth College. "Common Data Set 2023-2024." Dartmouth College Institutional Research. 2023.

Din, Kristine A. "Asian Pacific Islander Americans and Affirmative Negative Action." *The Vermont Connection* 33, no. 1 (2012).

Duke University. "Common Data Set 2023-2024." Duke University Institutional Research. 2023.

Duke University. "Common Data Set 2023-2024." Duke University Institutional Research. Accessed December 2024.

Espenshade, Thomas J., and Alexandria Walton Radford. *No Longer Separate, Not Yet Equal: Race and Class in Elite College Admission and Campus Life.* Princeton University Press, 2009.

Georgia Institute of Technology. "Common Data Set 2023-2024." Georgia Tech Office of Institutional Research and Planning. Accessed December 2024.

Harvard University. "Class of 2028 Admission Statistics." Harvard University Office of Undergraduate Admission. Accessed December 2024.

Harvard University. "Common Data Set 2023-2024." Harvard University Institutional Research. Accessed December 2024.

Kahneman, Daniel. *Thinking, Fast and Slow.* Farrar, Straus and Giroux, 2011.

Lucido, Jerome A. "The Marketing Student Search in American Higher Education." *New Directions for Student Services*, no. 118 (2007).

Massachusetts Institute of Technology. "Institutional Research Data." MIT Office of Institutional Research. Accessed December 2024.

Northwestern University. "Common Data Set 2023-2024." Northwestern University Institutional Research. 2023.

Park, Julie J. *Race on Campus: Debunking Myths with Data.* Harvard Education Press, 2018.

Pomona College. "Institutional Research Data." Pomona College Office of Institutional Research. Accessed December 2024.

The Princeton Review. *The Best 382 Colleges.* Princeton Review, 2017, Kindle edition.

Princeton University. "Common Data Set 2023-2024." Princeton University Office of Institutional Research. Accessed December 2024.

Stanford University. "Institutional Research Data." Stanford University Institutional Research. Accessed December 2024.

Stanford University. "Undergraduate Admission Facts 2023." Stanford University Office of Undergraduate Admission. 2023.

Steele, Claude M. "A Threat in the Air: How Stereotypes Shape Intellectual Identity and Performance." *American Psychologist* 52, no. 6 (1997).

Stevens, Mitchell L. *Creating a Class: College Admissions and the Education of Elites.* Harvard University Press, 2007.

Students for Fair Admissions, Inc. v. President and Fellows of Harvard College. 600 U.S. (2023).

Students for Fair Admissions, Inc. v. President and Fellows of Harvard College. Trial Exhibit P001 (2018).

University of California. "UC Admissions by the Numbers." UC Office of the President. 2021-2025.

University of California, Berkeley. "Common Data Set 2023-2024." UC Berkeley Office of Planning and Analysis. Accessed December 2024.

University of California, Los Angeles. "Common Data Set 2023-2024." UCLA Institutional Research. Accessed December 2024.

University of California, Los Angeles. "UCLA Admissions Statistics 2023." UCLA Undergraduate Admission. 2023.

University of Chicago. "Common Data Set 2023-2024." University of Chicago Institutional Research. Accessed December 2024.

University of Michigan. "Common Data Set 2023-2024." University of Michigan Office of Budget and Planning. Accessed December 2024.

University of Pennsylvania. "Common Data Set 2023-2024." Penn Institutional Research and Analysis. 2023.

University of Pennsylvania. "Common Data Set 2023-2024." Penn Institutional Research and Analysis. Accessed December 2024.

University of Virginia. "Common Data Set 2023-2024." UVA Institutional Research and Analytics. Accessed December 2024.

Williams College. "Common Data Set 2023-2024." Williams College Institutional Research. Accessed December 2024.

Yale University. "Common Data Set 2023-2024." Yale University Institutional Research. Accessed December 2024.

About the Author

BARBARA AUSTIN has devoted over thirty years to helping students gain admission to the nation's most selective colleges. For the past decade, she has specialized in working with Asian American students, developing innovative strategies to overcome the documented disadvantages they face in the admissions process. Her students have gained admission to every Ivy League university, Stanford, MIT, and dozens of other elite institutions.

Barbara is a published author of five previous books, including *Sad Nun at Synanon* (Holt), *Soulcatcher* (Holt), *Thin Within* (Double-day), and *Two to Four from 9 to 5* (Harper). In her most recent book, *50 Great Answers to the Most-Asked Questions on College Admissions* (College Quest Press), Barbara brings her storytelling expertise to the college application process. Published in 2025, it was the top-rated new college guide on Amazon.

Barbara's academic foundation includes a BA in English from Loyola Marymount, an MA in Creative Writing from San Francisco State University, and doctoral studies at both the Graduate Theological Union's conjoint program with UC Berkeley and the University of Integrative Learning, where she completed her dissertation on Process Philosophy and Creativity.

Barbara's teaching career spans tenure positions at San Francisco State University, Bowling Green State University, and Los Medanos College in Pittsburg, California.

In 1994, she founded College Quest, LLC, where she developed her highly successful approach. She focuses on helping students discover their authentic voices through writing "sticky essays" and creating meaningful impact through what she terms "remarkable projects."

Called one of the Bay Area's best-kept secrets by hundreds of grateful parents and students, Barbara has an extraordinary success rate in getting her students into top colleges. She now shares her proven methodology with a wider audience in *From Star to Superstar: The Asian American Guide to Elite Colleges*.

Barbara Austin can be reached at www.college-quest.com or barbara@college-quest.com.